# CHASING SUSTAINABILITY

## AN SDG JOURNEY THROUGH INDIA

ASHEER RAHMAN

# Contents

# Contents

# Preface

The adoption of the Sustainable Development Goals (SDGs) in 2015 marked a transformative milestone in global developmental efforts. Conceived during the United Nations General Assembly Summit, the SDGs build upon the success and limitations of their predecessor, the Millennium Development Goals (MDGs), which spanned from 2000 to 2015. While the MDGs prioritized poverty eradication and social development, the SDGs extend these ambitions with a comprehensive framework of 17 interconnected goals and 169 targets aimed at fostering inclusive growth, environmental sustainability, and social equity by 2030. The core principle of the SDGs—"Leave no one behind"—emphasizes inclusivity and equity in development.

The SDGs emerged as a response to the gaps and unmet needs identified during the MDG era. Although significant progress was made in areas such as poverty reduction and access to education, disparities persisted, necessitating a broader, integrated approach. Unlike the MDGs, which primarily addressed developing nations, the SDGs offer a universal agenda applicable to all countries, acknowledging the interconnected challenges of modern development—from climate change and biodiversity loss to inequality and urbanization.

The goals are structured around five thematic pillars:

1. People: End poverty and hunger in all forms, ensuring dignity and equality.

2. Planet: Protect natural resources and the climate for future generations.

3. Prosperity: Ensure prosperous and fulfilling lives in harmony with nature.

4. Peace: Foster peaceful, just, and inclusive societies.

5. Partnership: Mobilize global partnerships for sustainable development.

India, as a signatory to the 2030 Agenda, has committed to integrating the SDGs into its national development strategy. Given its size, population, and diversity, India's approach is crucial to the global achievement of these goals. The Government of India, led by NITI Aayog, functions as the nodal agency for SDG implementation, ensuring alignment with national policies such as the Vision 2030 document and sectoral strategies.

Despite India's proactive measures, several challenges impede SDG progress. These include:

1. Resource Constraints: Financing the SDGs requires substantial public and private investment, which remains unevenly distributed across states.
2. Data Gaps: Effective monitoring and evaluation are hindered by the absence of comprehensive, disaggregated data.
3. Policy Coherence: Ensuring alignment between national, state, and local policies is an ongoing challenge.
4. Stakeholder Engagement: Mobilizing diverse stakeholders, including civil society, the private sector, and local communities, requires sustained efforts and innovative partnerships.

India's demographic scale and economic trajectory make it a critical player in the global SDG agenda. For example, the state of Kerala provides an exemplary SDG localization model, leveraging its robust social indicators and participatory governance framework by integrating SDG initiatives into local governance structures. By addressing domestic challenges such as poverty, gender inequality, and environmental degradation, India can significantly contribute to global outcomes. Furthermore, its experiences in decentralized governance, technological innovation, and community-led initiatives offer valuable lessons for other countries.

Sustainable development is not just an aspiration—it is India's pathway to a resilient future. This book delves into the localization of the UN's Sustainable Development Goals (SDGs) through in-depth case studies across Indian states. By examining policies, challenges, and grassroots initiatives, it sheds light on India's progress toward an inclusive, sustainable tomorrow.

# CHAPTER ONE

# SDG 1 - No Poverty: A Case Study of Bihar

"Extreme poverty anywhere is a threat to human security everywhere." – Kofi Annan. Sustainable Development Goal 1 (SDG 1) aims to "End poverty in all its forms everywhere." India, as a signatory to the 2030 Agenda for Sustainable Development, has prioritized the eradication of poverty through multidimensional approaches that include improving health, education, social protection, and employment opportunities. Bihar, one of India's most populous states, presents a compelling case for understanding the complexities of poverty. Despite being rich in cultural heritage and human potential, Bihar has long struggled with poverty, underdevelopment, and the socio-economic challenges associated with them. This chapter explores the multi-dimensional aspects of poverty, and Bihar's progress under SDG 1, evaluates state and national policies, and presents recommendations informed by best practices from other states.

## *Poverty in Bihar*

Bihar's poverty is deeply entrenched, with the state ranking among the poorest in India. Over one-sixth of India's poor reside in Bihar. Studies reveal that rural Bihar suffers the highest levels of deprivation, with key districts like Araria facing multi-dimensional poverty. The stark inequality highlights the vulnerability of northern districts to climatic events such as floods, which exacerbate poverty cycles. Economic indicators paint a grim picture. Over 93% of Bihar's population can be classified as vulnerable. The primary drivers of poverty, as identified by Sharma (1995), include illiteracy, poor infrastructure, lack of employment opportunities, primitive agriculture, and systemic failures in governance.

## *Key Indicators for Poverty Eradication*

### Multidimensional Poverty

Bihar's high poverty rate is driven by low access to education, healthcare, and basic services. Rural areas are disproportionately affected, with over 60% of households lacking access to improved sanitation facilities. According to the National Multidimensional Poverty Index (MPI) 2021, Bihar had the highest multidimensional poverty rate in India, with over 51.91% of its population classified as multidimensionally poor (NITI Aayog, 2021). The Global Multidimensional Poverty Index (MPI) 2023 identifies low household income, lack of sanitation, and poor nutrition as critical deprivations affecting the state's population.

**Employment and Livelihoods**

Agriculture dominates Bihar's economy, employing over 70% of its workforce. High levels of unemployment and underemployment remain critical issues in Bihar. The Periodic Labour Force Survey (PLFS) 2022 reported that Bihar's unemployment rate stands at 8.9%, higher than the national average of 7.6%. Seasonal migration to other states is widespread due to the lack of local employment opportunities. Schemes like MGNREGS (Mahatma Gandhi National Rural Employment Guarantee Scheme) have provided employment to rural populations, yet implementation inefficiencies have limited their potential (Ministry of Rural Development, 2023).

**Health Insurance, Shelter and Social Protection Benefits**

A significant proportion of Bihar's population lacks access to adequate health insurance and housing. Limited access to health insurance schemes such as the Pradhan Mantri Jan Arogya Yojana (PMJAY) has exacerbated healthcare inequities in Bihar. The Pradhan Mantri Awas Yojana (PMAY) has facilitated the construction of over 2.5 million houses in the state (Ministry of Housing and Urban Affairs, 2023), yet a significant housing deficit remains. According to the Rural Health Statistics Report 2023, only 18% of rural households in Bihar have access to health insurance. Shelter inadequacies persist, with over 45% of rural households living in kutcha houses (Census 2011, updated projections). Access to social security schemes remains limited in rural Bihar, with gaps in implementation impacting the most vulnerable groups.

## *Causes of Poverty*

### 1. Structural Issues

Bihar's economy relies heavily on agriculture, yet poor irrigation facilities, frequent floods, and reliance on traditional methods hinder productivity. Land ownership remains skewed, leaving a majority of smallholders and agricultural laborers impoverished. Around 50–70% of wage earners lack access to nutritious food, stable housing, and essential assets.

### 2. Social Factors

Social inequalities, particularly gender disparities, further compound poverty. Women's exclusion from land rights and decision-making roles perpetuates cycles of poverty. Dr. Govind Kelkar emphasizes that empowering women through asset ownership and recognizing their labor in policies like MGNREGA can significantly shift socio-economic norms.

### 3. Migration

Out-migration is a defining characteristic of Bihar's rural economy. Research from the Institute for Human Development shows that nearly one-third of rural households depend on remittances from migrant labor. While this provides short-term relief, it often results in a lack of investment in local infrastructure and skill development.

# *Policies and Programs: National and State-Level Interventions*

1. **MGNREGS:** Bihar has benefited significantly from MGNREGS, which guarantees 100 days of wage employment annually. Despite operational challenges, the program has helped reduce seasonal migration by providing local employment opportunities (Ministry of Rural Development, 2023). While participation has increased, especially among women, poor childcare facilities and wage delays hinder its effectiveness.

2. **DAY-NULM (Deendayal Antyodaya Yojana-National Urban Livelihoods Mission):** This urban-focused initiative has empowered urban poor communities through skill training and self-employment. Bihar has successfully mobilized over 4,500 self-help groups (SHGs) under the program.

3. **PMAY (Pradhan Mantri Awas Yojana):** This scheme has improved access to affordable housing. Bihar received ₹10,000 crore in funding for constructing rural and urban housing under the PMAY in 2023.

4. **Atal Pension Yojana (APY):** The scheme has enhanced social security among Bihar's low-income workers. However, enrollment rates remain below the national average due to low awareness.

5. **National Social Assistance Programme (NSAP):** Bihar's implementation of old-age pensions and other social security benefits under the NSAP has been pivotal in addressing extreme poverty among senior citizens and widows.

6. **Public Distribution System (PDS):** Despite its universalization, issues like leakages and inefficient

delivery mechanisms limit its impact. A localized approach, as advocated by Jean Dreze, could improve outcomes.

7. **Integrated Child Development Services (ICDS) and Mid-Day Meal Scheme (MDMS):** These programs address malnutrition and educational access but require better fund utilization and monitoring.

## Community Initiatives

1. **JEEViKA (Bihar Rural Livelihoods Promotion Society):** JEEViKA has mobilized over 11 million rural women into self-help groups, facilitating their access to credit, entrepreneurship opportunities, and government schemes (World Bank, 2023).
2. **Community Sanitation Drives:** Initiatives under the Swachh Bharat Mission have improved sanitation coverage in Bihar, particularly through community-led total sanitation campaigns.
3. **Farmer Producer Organizations (FPOs):** Supported by the state government, these organizations have enhanced market access and income for smallholder farmers, contributing to poverty reduction.
4. **AI-Driven Governance:** Bihar has recently embraced AI-driven decision-support systems, enabling data-driven policymaking. According to NITI Aayog CEO B.V.R. Subrahmanyam, this marks a transformative phase in governance and service delivery.
5. **Women's Empowerment:** Initiatives like the Balika Cycle Yojana and microfinance through self-help groups (SHGs) have enhanced mobility and financial

independence among women. A 2018 evaluation of the Bihar Rural Livelihoods Project highlights the positive impact of low-cost credit in reducing rural indebtedness.

## *Recommendations and Best Practices*

1. **Skill Development and Employment Opportunities:** Tamil Nadu's Amma Skill Training Program offers a successful model for vocational training. Bihar could adopt similar initiatives to equip its workforce with market-relevant skills.
2. **Health Insurance Penetration:** Kerala's Karunya Arogya Suraksha Paddhathi/Comprehensive Health Insurance Scheme has achieved near-universal coverage. Bihar should prioritize awareness campaigns and expand insurance networks.
3. **Affordable Housing:** Maharashtra's Slum Rehabilitation Authority (SRA) model offers a replicable framework for addressing urban housing deficits.
4. **Technology-Driven Governance:** Andhra Pradesh's Real-Time Governance Society (RTGS) employs data analytics for efficient scheme implementation. Bihar could leverage such technologies for monitoring and evaluation.
5. **Climate-Resilient Agriculture:** Learning from Madhya Pradesh, which has promoted climate-resilient crops under the Pradhan Mantri Krishi Sinchayee Yojana (PMKSY), Bihar can strengthen its agricultural base.

## *Conclusion*

Bihar's journey toward achieving SDG 1 is characterized by both progress and persistent challenges. Multidimensional poverty, employment deficits, and housing inadequacies remain key barriers to development. However, the state's proactive policies, combined with national initiatives like MGNREGS and PMAY, have laid a strong foundation for poverty eradication. By adopting best practices from states like Tamil Nadu and Kerala, Bihar can accelerate its progress toward a poverty-free society. Achieving SDG 1 in Bihar is not merely a local imperative but a national and global priority, as the state's progress will significantly influence India's overall success in eradicating poverty by 2030. The words of Nitish Kumar, Bihar's Chief Minister, aptly summarize the vision: "Cash subsidies, universal food entitlements, and asset ownership should empower individuals, not just households, to rise above poverty. With collective will, Bihar will catch up with the rest of the country." By focusing on inclusive growth, innovative governance, and community-driven solutions, Bihar can overcome its challenges and emerge as a model for sustainable development.

# CHAPTER TWO

# SDG 2 – Zero Hunger: A Case Study on Jharkhand

Jharkhand, an eastern state of India, is characterized by a complex interplay of socio-economic and health-related challenges that contribute to significant malnutrition rates. The state has the highest prevalence of wasting and underweight and the third highest rate of stunting among children in India, along with alarmingly high anemia rates. Despite these severe challenges, Jharkhand exhibits a higher prevalence of exclusive breastfeeding compared to the national average. This paradox highlights the need to delve deeper into the immediate and underlying drivers of malnutrition in the region. The rural and tribal communities face higher rates of stunting, underweight, and anemia, exacerbated by factors such as gender discrimination, poverty, low education levels, and inadequate public health infrastructure. Districts like West Singhbhum stand out due to their extreme levels of malnutrition indicators, underscoring the urgent need for targeted interventions.

## *Socioeconomic and Cultural Factors Affecting Malnutrition in Jharkhand*

### Poverty and Food Insecurity

According to the State of Food Security and Nutrition in the World 2023, nearly 32% of the population in Jharkhand faces food insecurity. Eventhough 93.92 lakh people have escaped multidimensional poverty in Jharkhand till 2023, poverty continues to be a major cause of malnutrition in Jharkhand with 23.34% of the population living below the poverty line, the second highest in India. Economic constraints limit access to nutritious foods, leading to malnutrition. Lack of infrastructure and traditional practices sometimes affect present-day diets (Chaand, 2015). Many groups in the society are dependent on agriculture, which often fails to meet their nutritional needs. Delayed breastfeeding, inadequate cultural practices and lack of maternal nutritional education further exacerbate this problem (Dasgupta, Chaand, & Barla, 2018). Facilities, including Nutrition Rehabilitation Centres (NRCs), are limited. According to the CINI-USAID report (2012), remote areas of Jharkhand do not have adequate infrastructure to deal with the problem of malnutrition.

**Malnutrition and the intersectional factors affecting Malnutrition**

Malnutrition is common and important nutrients such as iron, protein and vitamins are often deficient. The National Family Health Survey (NFHS-5) (2019-21) highlights that 39.6% of children under five in Jharkhand are stunted, and 22.6% are wasted, both figures above the national averages. Additionally, 65.2% of women and 72.7% of children suffer from anaemia, reflecting critical nutritional gaps. A study by Brennan, McDonald and Shlomowitz (2004) suggested that malnutrition in states like Jharkhand can lead to undernourishment. For example, diarrhea, respiratory diseases and parasites can lead to malnutrition, leading to a vicious cycle of poor health and food insecurity.

Inequalities in education and information are increasing and lead to malnutrition. Challenges include inadequate breastfeeding and complementary practices, low awareness and a wide gap in mothers' knowledge and practices. The National Family Health Survey (NFHS) shows a worrying decline in cultural competence between the fourth and fifth rounds. The failure of the ICDS to meet the needs of the community is highlighted by the gap between demand and service. This lack of action has led to the breakdown of the nutritional support system needed to address malnutrition. Most parents use best practices, such as using starchy or softened milk substitutes during periods of slow breastfeeding. Negative beliefs, such as attributing pain to the "evil eye," can influence caregiving behavior and often delay treatment until the condition worsens. Mothers in the state face restrictions on making independent decisions about childcare, nutrition, and health care. Decisions about food and health are often made by older family members and men. Pregnant women and elderly women often follow strict dietary restrictions, which causes more discomfort for mothers and children.

**Agriculture, Climate and Social Factors**

Seasonal agriculture and erratic rainfall patterns lead to food insecurity. The Gross Value Added (GVA) from agriculture in the state grew at a modest rate of 2.6% annually between 2016-2022 (RBI, 2023). Gupta and Singh (2016) argue that household food insecurity remains a persistent problem due to low agricultural productivity and lack of diversity. Low fertility results in a combination of food scarcity (Blössner and Onis, 2005). Water leaks, inefficiencies and corruption in the (PDS) have contributed to the onset of malnutrition. These problems are particularly prevalent in rural and tribal areas. Low incomes and scarcity during the summer months make it difficult for families to trade. The Agricultural Census 2021 reveals that 80% of farmers in the state are small and marginal, limiting their capacity to adopt modern farming techniques. The staples of rice, dal and potatoes have little to do with adequate nutrition. Men's seasonal work outside the home weakens women, makes them responsible and delays their search for health.

Open defecation is common and there is no access to potable water or a safe water source. These conditions can lead to the spread of disease, which can have consequences for children's health and nutritional needs. Local Actors such as ASHA and AWCs play a key role in addressing malnutrition, but physical challenges also persist for them.

Distance from many villages makes it difficult for Nutrition Link Workers (NLW) to pitch in. Counseling efforts are often limited by language barriers, lack of training and inadequate community participation. Moreover, programs such as Community-Based Management of Acute Malnutrition (CMAM) operate in parallel with government efforts, leading to competition and ineffectiveness. Poor collaboration between health workers and community leaders disrupts services. The shift to new screening technologies like MUAC, puts pressure on frontline health workers to adapt to it. Inadequate follow-up care after discharging malnourished children, increasing the risk of relapses.

## *Critical Analysis of Government Schemes and Interventions aimed at tackling Malnutrition*

India has developed and implemented numerous schemes aimed at combating hunger and malnutrition, each designed to address different segments of society. While many of these schemes play vital roles in addressing hunger and malnutrition in India, challenges such as inefficiencies, corruption, and inconsistent implementation persist. Comprehensive reforms, including better targeting of beneficiaries, technological advancements, and rigorous oversight, are essential to ensuring these programs meet their objectives effectively.

**1. National Food Security Act (NFSA), 2013 and the Public Distribution System (PDS)**

Nearly 57% of Jharkhand's population benefits from subsidized food grains under the NFSA. The Public

Distribution System (PDS) is one of the largest food security programs globally, aimed at providing subsidized food grains to the economically disadvantaged. Implemented under the National Food Security Act (NFSA), it reaches 81.35 crore beneficiaries across India. This program ensures food grain distribution to 75% of rural and 50% of urban populations, with over 5.4 lakh fair price shops facilitating distribution. In Jharkhand, the extension of free food grain distribution under the Pradhan Mantri Garib Kalyan Anna Yojana for an additional five years, starting from January 2024, is also a welcome step. The PDS has significantly contributed to reducing food insecurity. However, challenges persist, such as delays in ration distribution, leakage, mismanagement, and corruption at the distribution level. The effectiveness of the scheme varies by region; rural areas face higher distribution inefficiencies compared to urban regions (Gupta and Singh 2016). Improvements such as digitization, direct benefit transfers (DBT), and stricter oversight could enhance its impact (Kumar 2007).

**2. Antyodaya Anna Yojana (AAY)/Pradhan Mantri Garib Kalyan Anna Yojana (PMGKAY)**

Launched in 2000, the Antyodaya Anna Yojana (AAY) targets the poorest of the poor, providing them with highly subsidized food grains. This scheme has been lauded for reaching vulnerable groups effectively and has been integrated into the Pradhan Mantri Garib Kalyan Anna Yojana (PMGKAY) since 2023. Yet, there are still gaps in implementation, such as incomplete beneficiary identification and inconsistent supply. Strengthening beneficiary verification and ensuring transparent allocation processes are necessary to maximize benefits.

**3. PM-KISAN (Pradhan Mantri Kisan Samman Nidhi)**

Over 35 lakh farmers in Jharkhand received income support under PM-KISAN, providing a financial safety net to enhance agricultural productivity (Ministry of Agriculture, 2023).

### 4. Soil Health Card Scheme

The initiative has promoted sustainable farming by providing personalized soil health recommendations to farmers. However, only 34% of the state's agricultural land has been covered so far (NITI Aayog, 2023).

### 5. National Livestock Mission

Livestock farming, a major livelihood source in Jharkhand, has benefited from subsidies and training programs. The mission has boosted income for rural households, particularly women-led dairy enterprises.

### 6. PM Fasal Bima Yojana

The crop insurance scheme has improved resilience among farmers against climate risks. However, low enrollment rates and delayed claim settlements hinder its effectiveness.

## *Maternal and Child Health Interventions*

### Antenatal Care (ANC)

Weight monitoring during pregnancy is a significant practice that helps healthcare providers assess maternal and fetal health. Consistent tracking of weight gains or losses can indicate nutritional adequacy, potential undernutrition, or other health issues that may need intervention. The receipt of Mother and Child Protection (MCP) cards further supports this monitoring process by facilitating the documentation and tracking of health services provided to the mother and child. These cards serve as a comprehensive record that aids healthcare providers and communities in coordinating care and ensuring that necessary services are delivered.

**Supplementation and Preventive Measures**

Maternal nutrition and health are bolstered through targeted supplementation and preventive measures. The use of iodized salt in households is a crucial intervention to prevent iodine deficiency disorders, which can have serious implications for both maternal and fetal health, including intellectual disabilities and developmental delays in children. Iron and Folic Acid (IFA) supplementation is essential for reducing anemia, which is common among pregnant women and can lead to fatigue, low immunity, and complications during childbirth.

Tetanus toxoid immunization is a preventative measure that protects both mothers and their newborns from neonatal tetanus, a potentially fatal condition. Deworming during pregnancy is another critical preventive step, as it mitigates the risks associated with intestinal parasites that can impair nutrient absorption and contribute to anemia. Additionally, the use of mosquito nets is an effective measure to prevent malaria, which poses significant risks to pregnant women and their unborn children, potentially leading to complications such as low birth weight and preterm birth.

Health and nutrition education during pregnancy encourages mothers to adopt healthy eating habits,including colostrum feeding and understand the importance of hydration, and take necessary precautions for optimal health. These educational sessions foster long-term behavior changes that can contribute to the well-being of both mother and child.

**Institutional and Financial Support**

Institutional births, facilitated by skilled birth attendants, are a key factor in reducing maternal and neonatal mortality. The presence of trained healthcare professionals ensures safer childbirth practices, immediate postnatal care, and early interventions if complications arise. Financial assistance programs such as the Janani Suraksha Yojana (JSY) encourage institutional deliveries by reducing the financial burden on families and improving access to quality maternal healthcare.

Postnatal care for mothers and babies is equally vital, as it allows for the early detection of post-delivery complications, such as infections, excessive bleeding, or lactation issues. Continued support during the postnatal period helps to ensure recovery and promote bonding between the mother and child.

**Early Childhood Nutrition and Health**

Early childhood is a critical period for growth and development, and addressing nutritional needs is fundamental for ensuring long-term health. Food supplementation for children aged 6-35 months is an effective strategy to combat dietary deficiencies that contribute to malnutrition. This targeted intervention can help bridge nutritional gaps, improving the overall health and development of young children.

Vitamin A supplementation is another vital component, as it enhances immunity and reduces the risk of blindness in children. Pediatric iron and folic acid (IFA) supplementation, along with deworming, are essential for combating anemia and parasitic infections that can stunt growth and impair cognitive development. Full immunization coverage protects against common childhood diseases, contributing to reduced mortality rates and enhanced child health.

## Growth Monitoring and Counseling

Routine weighing and growth counseling are crucial for tracking and supporting a child's development. Regular growth assessments help identify deviations from normal growth patterns, enabling timely interventions to prevent further complications. Preschool education at Anganwadi Centers (AWCs) also plays a significant role in enhancing cognitive and social skills, preparing children for future academic and personal success.

## Mission POSHAN and other programs

With key schemes like POSHAN Abhiyaan, Anganwadi Services, and the Scheme for Adolescent Girls, building upon the existing Anganwadi Services and introducing new schemes like Poshan Vatikas (Nutri-gardens) to make fruits, vegetables, and medicinal plants more accessible, these programs provide hot cooked meals and take-home rations to million with around 14 lakh Anganwadi centers reaching approximately 10 crore beneficiaries, including 8.87 crore children under six and 1.1 crore pregnant and lactating mothers.

The Mid-Day Meal Scheme, initiated in 1995, aims to improve nutritional levels and encourage school attendance among children. Studies have shown its positive impact on reducing malnutrition and improving school enrollment rates (Brennan, McDonald, and Shlomowitz 2004). The Pradhan Mantri Poshan Shakti Nirman (PM POSHAN) is recognized as the world's largest school feeding program, designed to tackle the dual challenges of enhancing children's nutritional status and boosting school enrollment. The scheme provides hot, cooked meals to children in preschools or Bal Vatikas (before class I) as well as to 11.80 crore children in classes I to VIII across 11.20 lakh schools. However, issues such as poor food quality, inadequate infrastructure, and regional disparities limit its effectiveness. Comprehensive training for staff and increased funding for infrastructure could address these challenges.

The ICDS program, launched in 1975, provides comprehensive services including nutrition, health, and education for children under six and their mothers. The scheme has shown significant strides in improving child health and nutrition, especially through its Anganwadi centers. Nonetheless, gaps remain due to inconsistent service delivery and resource shortages. Ensuring regular training for Anganwadi workers and enhancing community engagement can bolster the scheme's reach and efficiency.

## Community Initiatives

1. **Sahiyans (Community Health Workers):** These workers play a vital role in addressing malnutrition in rural Jharkhand by promoting breastfeeding, distributing iron supplements, and raising awareness about balanced diets.
2. **Women's Self-Help Groups (SHGs):** SHGs under the Jharkhand State Livelihood Promotion Society (JSLPS) have empowered women through livelihood diversification, particularly in poultry farming and food processing.

## Recommendations

1. **Improving Nutrition** : Kerala's Kudumbashree initiative, which empowers women through nutrition gardens, can serve as a model for improving household-level food security in Jharkhand. Puducherry's universal Anganwadi system also demonstrates the importance of robust early childhood nutrition programs. Customized programs focusing on the nutritional and livelihood needs of tribal populations, as implemented in Odisha, can help bridge disparities.

2. **Strengthening Food Distribution and Agricultural Productivity** : Jharkhand should adopt Tamil Nadu's smart Public Distribution System (PDS) to minimize leakages and improve last-mile delivery of subsidized food grains. Jharkhand can also emulate Madhya Pradesh's crop diversification programs, which have increased farmers' incomes by promoting high-value crops. Adoption of climate-smart agriculture practices, as implemented in Gujarat, can mitigate the risks associated with climate variability.

3. **Health Worker Engagement:** Regular counseling sessions led by health workers for pregnancy and early childhood provide continuous support and education to families. Health workers also educate communities on maintaining hygiene, adopting nutritional practices, and preventing common illnesses. Promoting household-level practices, such as the use of iodized salt and mosquito nets, helps prevent nutritional deficiencies and protect against malaria. Counseling on hygiene and nutrition empowers families to adopt habits that contribute to overall health and well-being.

4. **Financial and Logistical Support:** Financial incentives for institutional deliveries and postnatal care encourage families to seek professional medical support. Access

to supplementary nutrition and healthcare services through AWCs ensures that vulnerable groups receive the necessary support to thrive.

### Other Recommendations

Strengthening community outreach through health workers and AWCs can bridge knowledge gaps and encourage the adoption of healthy practices. Enhancing the coverage and quality of ANC and postnatal care will ensure comprehensive maternal and child health support. Promoting nutrition and preventive healthcare education is critical for empowering communities. Increasing financial and infrastructural support for institutional care will enable broader access to essential services, ultimately improving health outcomes.

## *Conclusion*

Efforts by Jharkhand to address malnutrition, including the establishment of a dedicated nutrition mission and various multi-sectoral schemes, have shown incremental improvements in nutrition coverage. However, significant challenges remain, such as inconsistent fund utilization, inadequate infrastructure, and limited reach of critical services like antenatal care and micronutrient supplementation. The state's focus on nutritional interventions must be reinforced with increased budget allocation, decentralized planning, and improved public health infrastructure, particularly in rural and tribal areas. Addressing these gaps will require sustained investment, capacity building, and a holistic approach involving the cooperation of various state departments and community-based organizations. With targeted measures and strengthened implementation strategies, Jharkhand can make substantial progress toward eradicating malnutrition and ensuring a healthier future for its population.

# SDG 3 – Good Health and Well-Being: A Case Study on Chhattisgarh

Sustainable Development Goal 3 (SDG 3) emphasizes ensuring healthy lives and promoting well-being for people of all ages. Chhattisgarh, a tribal-dominated state, faces significant challenges in healthcare delivery due to geographic remoteness, limited infrastructure, and socio-economic disparities. Despite these obstacles, the state has made notable strides in healthcare access and outcomes. This chapter delves into Chhattisgarh's progress toward achieving SDG 3 by analyzing key health indicators, policy initiatives, community efforts, and areas for improvement while drawing on best practices from other states like Kerala, Tamil Nadu, and Andhra Pradesh.

## *Key Health Indicators*

### Immunization Coverage
As per NFHS-5 (2019-21), Chhattisgarh's full immunization coverage for children aged 12-23 months stood at 88.5%, higher than the national average of 76.4%.

### Malnutrition and Public Health
Chhattisgarh struggles with high malnutrition rates, particularly among children under five. While government schemes like the Mukhyamantri Suposhan Yojana have made strides, the problem persists, especially in tribal populations.

### Maternal Mortality Rate (MMR)

The state's MMR has significantly reduced from 246 per lakh live births in 2013 to 141 in 2021 (NITI Aayog, 2023). Programs like the Pradhan Mantri Surakshit Matritva Abhiyan (PMSMA) have contributed to improved maternal health.

### Infant Mortality Rate (IMR)

Chhattisgarh's IMR is 38 per 1,000 live births, higher than the national average of 28. Innovative measures like Janani Suraksha Yojana (JSY) have improved institutional deliveries but challenges persist.

**Anaemia**

Anaemia remains a pressing issue, with 65% of women aged 15-49 years and 70.7% of children under five affected (NFHS-5). The Anaemia Mukt Bharat Abhiyan has been instrumental in addressing this.

**Communicable and Non-Communicable Diseases**

Chhattisgarh's dual burden of communicable and non-communicable diseases further complicates its health landscape. Malaria, in particular, is endemic in the tribal belts. Reports of drug-resistant strains further complicate disease management. The state has recorded a tuberculosis (TB) prevalence rate of 210 per 1,00,000 population. Programs under the National Tuberculosis Elimination Program (NTEP) have made incremental progress. HIV prevalence remains low at 0.23%, supported by targeted interventions for high-risk groups. Meanwhile, the rising prevalence of non-communicable diseases such as diabetes and hypertension reflects an epidemiological transition.

**Life Expectancy**

Life expectancy at birth in Chhattisgarh is 64.8 years, lower than the national average of 69.6 years, reflecting systemic healthcare challenges (MOSPI, 2023).

**Health Insurance**

Under Ayushman Bharat - Pradhan Mantri Jan Arogya Yojana (AB-PMJAY), over 52 lakh families in Chhattisgarh

are enrolled, ensuring financial protection for healthcare.
**Healthcare Workforce**

The state has 25.9 skilled health workers per 10,000 population, below the WHO recommendation of 44.5. Increasing the health workforce in rural areas is critical.

## *Challenges*

1. **Healthcare Coverage**: The state's healthcare infrastructure remains inadequate, with a severe shortage of primary health centers (PHCs) and community health centers (CHCs). Geographic isolation and inadequate infrastructure hinder healthcare delivery in tribal belts. There is a significant deficit in trained healthcare professionals. Rural areas face acute shortages of auxiliary nurse midwives (ANMs) and paramedics, exacerbating disparities.
2. **Social Factors**: Poverty and illiteracy among tribal populations also impede their access to healthcare. Early marriages and adolescent pregnancies contribute to poor maternal and child health outcomes. Cultural and social norms further constrain access to health services. Limited awareness about preventive healthcare and family planning restricts health-seeking behaviors.
3. **Low Health Expenditure**: Chhattisgarh allocates only 4% of its GDP to healthcare, insufficient to meet the growing demands.

## *Policies and Programs: National and State Initiatives*

1. **National Health Mission (NHM):** NHM has strengthened primary healthcare by establishing Health and Wellness Centres (HWCs) in rural areas. Chhattisgarh has operationalized over 3,500 HWCs, providing essential services like maternal and child health. Yet its impact is limited by staffing shortages and infrastructure constraints.

2. **Ayushman Bharat - Pradhan Mantri Jan Arogya Yojana (AB-PMJAY):** The scheme covers 5 lakh per family per year for secondary and tertiary care, benefiting marginalized communities.

3. **Pradhan Mantri Matru Vandana Yojana (PMMVY):** PMMVY provides cash incentives to pregnant women for safe motherhood. Over 4 lakh beneficiaries have been enrolled in Chhattisgarh (MOSPI, 2023).

4. **Poshan Abhiyan:** Aimed at reducing stunting and malnutrition, 1.5 lakh Anganwadi workers in Chhattisgarh implement nutritional interventions targeting women and children.

5. **Jan Suraksha Yojana:** Focused on accident and disability insurance, this scheme provides financial protection to vulnerable groups.

6. **Pradhan Mantri Jan Aushadhi Yojana (PMJAY):** The state operates 350 Jan Aushadhi Kendras, offering affordable generic medicines to reduce out-of-pocket medical expenses.

7. **Mukhyamantri Haat Bazar Clinic Yojana and Dai-Didi Clinics** have improved healthcare access for women and remote communities.

8. The **Mukhyamantri Suposhan Yojana** has targeted malnutrition but requires integration with education and sanitation initiatives for holistic impact.

## *Community Initiatives*

1. **Mitanin Program:** Chhattisgarh's Mitanin program, modeled on community health workers, has been pivotal in delivering healthcare services to remote tribal areas. These women health volunteers are the backbone of the state's primary healthcare system. The Rural Medical Assistant scheme and Phulwari centers also aim to enhance healthcare delivery in underserved regions.
2. **Telemedicine Services:** Implementation of initiatives like the e-Sanjeevani telemedicine platform bridge healthcare gaps in remote regions, providing consultations to over 1 lakh patients annually.
3. **Nutrition Rehabilitation Centers (NRCs):** NRCs cater to malnourished children by offering specialized care and nutritional counseling to families.

## *Recommendations and Best Practices*

1. **Strengthening Primary Healthcare:** Kerala's robust Primary Health Centres and Family Health Centers (FHCs) can serve as a model for improving primary care in rural areas of Chhattisgarh.
2. **Improving Maternal Health:** Tamil Nadu's Dr. Muthulakshmi Reddy Maternity Benefit Scheme, which

offers cash incentives for institutional deliveries, can be adopted.

3. **Enhancing Immunization:** Intensified Mission Indradhanush introduced in states like Andhra Pradesh demonstrates the effectiveness of targeted immunization drives.

4. **Reducing Out-of-Pocket Expenditure:** Expanding the coverage of PM Jan Arogya Yojana and ensuring free access to essential medicines can alleviate financial burdens on families.

5. **Recruiting Healthcare Workers:** Innovative recruitment strategies, as adopted in Rajasthan, can address the shortage of skilled health workers in underserved areas.

## *Conclusion*

Chhattisgarh has made significant progress in improving healthcare access and outcomes, yet considerable challenges remain in achieving SDG 3. Corruption, logistical inefficiencies, and lack of localized solutions hinder the effectiveness of policy implementation. By leveraging national and state-level policies, strengthening community-based interventions, and adopting best practices from other states, the state can accelerate its journey toward universal healthcare. A holistic approach emphasizing preventive care, robust infrastructure, and targeted nutritional interventions will be essential for achieving quality health and well-being for all in Chhattisgarh.

# CHAPTER FOUR

# SDG 4 – Quality Education: A Case Study on Bihar and Odisha

Sustainable Development Goal 4 (SDG 4) seeks to ensure inclusive and equitable quality education and promote lifelong learning opportunities for all. Education is fundamental to breaking the cycle of poverty, fostering social justice, and achieving sustainable development. Bihar and Odisha, two Indian states with varying socio-economic landscapes, face unique challenges in their efforts to achieve SDG 4. This chapter examines their progress through key education indicators, policy interventions, and community-driven initiatives. Furthermore, the chapter highlights best practices from other states, offering actionable recommendations for both Bihar and Odisha.

## *Key Indicators of Education*

### Enrollment Rates

Enrollment rates reflect a state's ability to provide access to education across different levels. With a Gross Enrollment Ratio (GER) of 95.2% at the primary level (Classes 1–5), the state has made strides in universal access. However, the GER drops drastically to 60.4% at the secondary level (Classes 9–12), indicating systemic issues such as high dropout rates and inadequate school infrastructure (SDG India Index, 2023-24). Odisha fares better, with a GER of 96.8% at the primary level and 78.9% at the secondary level. This relatively better performance is attributed to targeted state policies and community engagement in rural education initiatives.

### Literacy and Numeracy

Bihar's literacy rate stands at 61.8%, the lowest among Indian states. Gender disparities are stark, with male literacy at 71.2% and female literacy at 51.5% (NSSO, 2023). Limited access to secondary education and socio-economic barriers contribute to these gaps. Odisha exhibits a higher literacy rate of 77.3%, with male literacy at 82.4% and female literacy at 72.9%. While the gender gap is narrower than Bihar, tribal and rural populations still face significant challenges in literacy attainment.

### Dropout Rates

High dropout rates hinder the achievement of SDG 4 in both states. In Bihar, the dropout rate at the secondary level is 15.9%, attributed to factors such as child labor, early marriages, and lack of transportation facilities in rural areas. Odisha's dropout rate is lower at 10.4%, supported by state-led initiatives like scholarships and free textbooks. However, challenges remain for tribal communities, where cultural and linguistic barriers affect retention.

### Gender Parity Index (GPI)

GPI measures the ratio of females to males enrolled in educational institutions. Bihar's GPI at the primary level is 0.96, indicating near parity. However, GPI declines at higher levels due to social norms restricting girls' education. Odisha achieves a GPI of 0.98 at the primary level, reflecting consistent efforts to close the gender gap through campaigns like the "Beti Bachao Beti Padhao" initiative.

### Pupil-Teacher Ratio (PTR)

For Bihar, PTR is 43:1, significantly exceeding the national norm of 30:1. This shortfall is compounded by a lack of qualified teachers, particularly in rural and semi-urban areas. For Odisha, PTR stands at 27:1, demonstrating better teacher deployment. However, rural schools still face challenges in retaining experienced educators.

## *Key Policies and Programs*

### National Initiatives

1. Right to Education (RTE) Act, 2009: Mandates free and compulsory education for children aged 6–14. Both Bihar and Odisha have made progress in improving enrollment and attendance under RTE. However, infrastructural gaps like the absence of functional toilets and libraries persist, particularly in Bihar.
2. Samagra Shiksha Abhiyan (SSA): This umbrella scheme integrates earlier programs like SSA and RMSA to provide holistic education. Funds have been utilized in

both states to improve school infrastructure, teacher training, and digital learning tools.

3. PM POSHAN (Mid-Day Meal Scheme): Over 20 million children in Bihar and 8.7 million in Odisha benefit from the scheme. In addition to improving attendance, it has significantly addressed malnutrition among school-aged children.

4. Eklavya Model Residential Schools (EMRS): Odisha leads in the implementation of EMRS, operating 35 schools for tribal students. Bihar is in the early stages of adopting this model.

5. Rashtriya Avishkar Abhiyan (RAA): Both states are working to enhance STEM education through RAA. Odisha has integrated local initiatives to promote innovation and technical skills in schools.

**State-Specific Initiatives**

1. **The Mukhyamantri Balika Cycle Yojana** in Bihar provides bicycles to girls, increasing retention rates and reducing gender disparities in secondary education.

2. **Unnayan Bihar, is a digital education initiative** using mobile apps and video content to support rural students.

3. **The Mo School Campaign** in Odisha mobilizes alumni to contribute to school development, raising over ₹300 crore.

4. **KALIA Scholarships** in Odisha offers financial aid to children of farmers pursuing higher education.

## *Challenges in Quality Education*

**Infrastructure Deficiencies and Teacher Shortages in Bihar**

Over 20% of schools lack functional toilets, and only 38% have electricity (U-DISE, 2023). Approximately 30% of teacher positions remain vacant, affecting student outcomes and learning continuity.

**Tribal and Digital Divide in Odisha**

Language barriers and socio-economic constraints contribute to low retention rates among tribal students. Limited internet penetration in rural areas affects the effectiveness of digital education programs like Unnayan Bihar.

## *Community Initiatives*

1. **Learning Camps:** NGOs like Pratham have conducted learning camps in both states, significantly improving foundational literacy and numeracy skills.
2. **Village Education Committees (VECs):** These committees empower local communities in Odisha to oversee school development plans under Samagra Shiksha.

**Recommendations and Best Practices**

In the case of Infrastructure Development, Kerala's Model of Investment in libraries, ICT labs, and smart classrooms can address the infrastructure gaps in both Bihar and Odisha. Following Delhi's Teacher Development Program with its regular capacity-building initiatives can enhance teacher performance in both states. For Tribal Education, the model of Madhya Pradesh's Multi-Lingual Education Program may be looked at for implementing local-language instruction can improve retention among tribal students in Odisha. Using Andhra Pradesh's AP Janmabhoomi model, community-driven digital literacy campaigns can bridge the digital divide in Bihar. Vocational training centers under the STRIVE scheme can focus on local employability, especially in rural regions.

## *Conclusion*

Bihar and Odisha have shown commendable efforts toward achieving SDG 4, but significant challenges remain. Addressing issues such as high dropout rates, gender disparities, and infrastructure deficits requires a holistic and inclusive approach. By leveraging successful national programs, state-specific policies, and best practices from other regions, both states can create an equitable and effective education system that supports long-term sustainable development.

# CHAPTER FIVE

# SDG 5 – Gender Equality: A Case Study on Uttar Pradesh

"Where a woman is respected, prosperity thrives", yet Uttar Pradesh, the most populous state in India, tells a more complex story. In the SDG India Index 2023-2024, Uttar Pradesh (UP) continues to grapple with severe gender inequality, earning its place alongside Bihar and Madhya Pradesh in lagging behind on SDG 5: Gender Equality. Through the lens of stark realities, systemic barriers, and cautious hope, this chapter unpacks the intertwined narratives of health, education, and empowerment in Uttar Pradesh's journey toward gender equality.

## *CHALLENGES*

**Poverty, Malnutrition and Maternal Health**

Picture a young girl in a rural district of UP, her dreams of a brighter tomorrow dimmed by persistent malnutrition. Programs like the Integrated Child Development Services (ICDS), intended to be her lifeline, struggle to provide holistic solutions. Disconnected efforts between departments mean that nutritional needs are often treated in isolation, leaving many women and adolescent girls vulnerable to poor health outcomes. In the agricultural fields, countless women toil under the sun, yet their contributions remain invisible. Their labor is unrecognized, their voices unheard, and incentives nonexistent. This neglect exacerbates an already dire situation, perpetuating cycles of poverty and malnutrition.

From childhood, the gender disparity becomes evident. UP's sex ratio falls below the national average, emblematic of deeply entrenched social biases. For many girls, life becomes a countdown to marriage, often before reaching adulthood. In places like Shravasti, where the infant mortality rate is among the highest in the country, early marriage and poor maternal health collide with devastating consequences.

**Economic Factors**

The female labor force participation rate (LFPR) in UP is a mere 16.1%, significantly lower than the national average of 22.8% (Periodic Labour Force Survey, 2022). Cultural norms and safety concerns heavily restrict women's entry into the workforce. Female illiteracy compounds these issues, locking girls in a cycle of limited opportunity, dependency, and unrealized potential. Across rural UP, women's economic empowerment is stifled by their exclusion from land ownership. Although they form the backbone of agricultural labor, women rarely own the land they till, robbing them of economic security and decision-making power.

In rural UP, the story of economic empowerment is one of slow but steady progress. A 2022 study by the V.V. Giri National Labour Institute highlights small victories—more women accessing banking services, owning mobile phones, and participating in government schemes. Yet, the absence of meaningful land rights and modern farming tools underscores the vast distance still to be traveled.

**Social Factors**

Even in governance, where women are ostensibly gaining representation, the shadow of patriarchy looms. The "Pradhan Pati" phenomenon—where elected female leaders act as proxies for their male relatives—turns political empowerment into a hollow gesture.

At the heart of UP's gender inequality lies a pervasive cultural preference for sons. Studies reveal that over half of uneducated men in the state harbor a strong preference for male children, with similar attitudes mirrored among uneducated women. Such attitudes are reinforced by patriarchal norms that confine women to the domestic sphere.

The state's child marriage rate stands at 16.6%, significantly impacting education and health outcomes for girls. Rural areas report higher prevalence due to poverty and lack of awareness (NFHS-5, 2019-21).

**Violence Against Women**

According to NFHS-5 (2019-21), 42% of women in UP have experienced some form of spousal violence, higher than the national average of 29.3%. UP consistently records the highest number of reported cases of crimes against women, including dowry deaths and acid attacks (NCRB, 2022). This is indicative of deep-rooted patriarchal attitudes. For those daring to dream beyond these boundaries, the road is fraught with challenges, from early marriage to systemic violence. National Family Health Survey data underscores the issue: 42% of ever-married women in UP report having faced physical or sexual violence—higher than the national average.

UP remains a hotspot for trafficking, particularly of young girls for labor and sexual exploitation. Approximately 22% of trafficking cases in India originate in UP (Ministry of Home Affairs, 2022).

**Gap in Education**

Education emerges as both a challenge and a solution. The Gender Parity Index (GPI) for primary education is 0.95, which declines to 0.84 at the secondary level, highlighting dropouts among adolescent girls due to societal expectations and safety issues (SDG India Index, 2023-24). Programs like Padhein Betiyan Badhein Betiyan and the Adult Literacy Programme aim to elevate educational outcomes for women and girls. Research by Dostie and Jayaraman (2006) emphasizes that parental education, particularly mothers', significantly increases girls' enrollment in schools. However, infrastructure gaps, patriarchal attitudes, and economic pressures continue to hold many back. In districts like Awadh's northern region, as noted by Bano (2017), gender disparity in literacy remains stark. For these girls, education is more than a right—it is a lifeline to escape systemic oppression.

Hope arrives in the form of state-led initiatives like Kanya Sumangala Yojana, which supports girls at crucial life stages, and Beti Bachao Beti Padhao, aimed at curbing gender-based violence and promoting education. However, these schemes face the challenge of inadequate implementation. Without interdepartmental coordination and community engagement, these well-meaning efforts often fail to achieve their full impact.

Rural educational disparities are glaring. In districts like Jaunpur, literacy levels among women remain strikingly low. Factors such as inadequate school facilities, long distances, and societal expectations that girls prioritize household duties over education keep many out of classrooms.

## *ANALYSIS OF GOVERNMENT POLICIES*

An analysis of Central Government schemes aimed at achieving gender equality reveals numerous schemes to address gender disparities, empowering women through education, health, financial inclusion, and social support. While these initiatives are ambitious, their success often hinges on effective implementation, addressing socio-cultural barriers, and ensuring comprehensive outreach. Below is a critical analysis of key schemes, highlighting their achievements and challenges.

**1. Beti Bachao Beti Padhao (BBBP)**

Launched in 2015, BBBP aims to address the declining child sex ratio and promote girl child education. The scheme has succeeded in raising awareness about gender equality, as reflected in improved sex ratios in states like Haryana. However, a 2018 Comptroller and Auditor General (CAG) report revealed that 56% of funds were used for publicity campaigns rather than ground-level interventions, limiting its impact. Moreover, the lack of coordination among implementing agencies has diluted its effectiveness (Chaudhary, 2020).

### 2. Sukanya Samriddhi Yojana (SSY)

The Sukanya Samriddhi Yojana, launched in 2015, encourages parents to save for their daughters' education and marriage through tax-free savings accounts. While the scheme has seen significant participation, its benefits are often limited to middle-income families with access to banking services. Rural areas with financial illiteracy and limited banking penetration have lower enrollment rates, undermining its inclusivity (Kumar & Mishra, 2019).

### 3. Janani Suraksha Yojana (JSY)

As part of the National Health Mission, JSY incentivizes institutional deliveries to reduce maternal and infant mortality. The scheme has been instrumental in increasing institutional deliveries, particularly among economically disadvantaged women. However, delays in disbursing cash incentives and inadequate healthcare infrastructure in rural areas remain significant hurdles (Basu et al., 2021).

### 4. Pradhan Mantri Mudra Yojana (PMMY)

This scheme provides collateral-free loans to small businesses, with a special focus on women entrepreneurs. As of 2023, women constituted 68% of Mudra loan beneficiaries, reflecting the program's success in encouraging female entrepreneurship. However, the loans are often used for low-income ventures with minimal profit margins, limiting their transformative potential (Nair, 2020). Additionally, many women lack the business training needed to utilize loans effectively.

### 5. Kasturba Gandhi Balika Vidyalaya (KGBV)

Launched in 2004, KGBV provides residential schooling for girls from marginalized communities. The scheme has played a crucial role in reducing dropout rates and ensuring secondary education for girls in rural areas. However, challenges such as poor infrastructure, insufficient funding, and teacher shortages have hindered its full potential (Mishra & Gupta, 2022).

### 6. Pragati Scholarship Scheme

This scholarship aims to support girls pursuing technical education, such as engineering and technology. While the scheme has helped improve female enrollment in STEM courses, awareness about it remains low, especially in rural and semi-urban areas. Furthermore, institutional biases against women in STEM careers often undermine its long-term impact (Sharma, 2021).

### 7. One Stop Centre (OSC)

Established to support women facing violence, OSCs provide integrated services, including legal aid, psychological support, and shelter. As of 2023, over 1,000 centers were operational. While OSCs have provided critical support, their accessibility is limited in rural and remote areas. A 2020 study by Menon et al. revealed that many such centres lack trained counselors and adequate funding, reducing their effectiveness.

### 8. Women's Helpline (181)

The 181 Women's Helpline offers 24/7 support to women facing violence or distress. While the helpline has been a lifeline for many, frequent technical glitches, lack of trained operators, and delays in action have diminished its reliability (Rao, 2021). Moreover, societal stigma often discourages women from reporting abuse, limiting the helpline's utilization.

## Community Initiatives

Programs under the National Rural Livelihoods Mission (NRLM) have empowered over 6 lakh women in UP through SHGs, fostering financial independence and community leadership. SHGs in districts like Gorakhpur and Varanasi have successfully mobilized women to address issues like domestic violence and child marriage. NGOs like Educate Girls organize camps to reduce dropout rates among adolescent girls in rural UP, achieving an 80% re-enrollment rate in targeted districts. Initiatives like the Mahila Samakhya Program involve women in addressing local safety concerns, creating safer environments for girls to pursue education and employment.

## Recommendations and Best Practices

Nagaland's Women's Societies implement community-driven mechanisms to mediate domestic disputes and prevent violence. Kerala's Kudumbashree Mission has established women-led micro-enterprises to enhance financial independence and skill development. Lakshadweep's Crime-Free Model adopts stringent local governance measures to ensure women's safety. Delhi's School Safety Program incorporates safety audits and gender sensitization workshops in schools. Rajasthan's Udaan Initiative may be looked into for mobilizing community leaders and providing conditional cash transfers to discourage early marriages. Andhra Pradesh's e-Pragati Program model can bridge the digital divide by promoting digital literacy among rural women through free training and subsidized mobile devices. Providing creche facilities and flexible working hours such as under Tamil Nadu's Amma Creche Scheme and incentivizing private sector participation in gender diversity programs can enhance workforce participation.

## *Conclusion*

Uttar Pradesh's struggle with gender inequality is not just a challenge of policy but of perception. Entrenched patriarchy, insufficient resources, and fragmented implementation have hindered progress. Yet, the path forward is not without hope. India's gender equality schemes reflect a commendable commitment to SDG 5, addressing challenges in health, education, financial inclusion, and violence prevention. However, the overarching issue lies in implementation gaps, insufficient awareness, and socio-cultural barriers. For these schemes to achieve their intended outcomes, the government must improve coordination among implementing agencies, ensure equitable rural outreach and address societal biases through sustained awareness campaigns.

Gender equality cannot be achieved through isolated efforts; it requires systemic reform, grassroots participation, and continuous evaluation to ensure no woman is left behind. By fostering coordinated action across departments, ensuring the effective implementation of existing schemes, and promoting education and economic empowerment, UP can begin to close the gender gap. It requires a collective effort—a recognition that achieving SDG 5 is not just about equality for women, but progress for all.

# SDG 6 – Clean Water and Sanitation: A Case Study on Rajasthan

Access to clean water and sanitation remains a significant challenge in India, especially in rural and underserved regions. Rajasthan, a desert state with a rapidly growing population, faces considerable hurdles in achieving SDG 6 (Clean Water and Sanitation). This chapter evaluates Rajasthan's performance in this area, focusing on key indicators, current policies, challenges, and recommendations.

## Key Indicators and Performance in Rajasthan

Rajasthan, according to the India SDG Index, has made gradual progress in the provision of clean water and sanitation, yet continues to struggle with key performance indicators (KPIs) under SDG 6. The state's performance is assessed across several parameters, including access to drinking water, sanitation facilities, and wastewater management.

1. **Drinking Water Access:** As of the latest reports, around 85% of Rajasthan's rural households have access to basic drinking water services, a significant improvement compared to previous years. However, many of these sources are unreliable or contaminated, particularly in remote desert and arid regions where groundwater levels are depleting rapidly (NITI Aayog, 2020; Department of Drinking Water and Sanitation, 2021).

2. **Sanitation Facilities:** According to the Swachh Bharat Mission (SBM), Rajasthan has made substantial strides in improving sanitation, with over 85% of rural households having access to toilets. However, the quality and maintenance of sanitation facilities remain

inconsistent, with many rural areas still practicing open defecation (NITI Aayog, 2020).

3. **Wastewater Treatment:** Wastewater management remains a challenge, with most of the state's wastewater either untreated or poorly treated before being discharged into natural water bodies, further exacerbating water pollution (Department of Drinking Water and Sanitation, 2021).

## Current National and State Policies and Schemes

Several policies and government programs aim to improve water and sanitation in Rajasthan:

**National Policies and Schemes**

1. Swachh Bharat Mission (SBM): The Swachh Bharat Mission (SBM), launched in 2014, has played a pivotal role in enhancing sanitation in India, including in Rajasthan. SBM's rural component aims to achieve a clean and open-defecation-free India by promoting household toilets, rural sanitation infrastructure, and behavior change programs. Rajasthan has shown notable progress, with a large proportion of rural households receiving access to toilets. However, maintaining and ensuring their functionality remains a challenge in many regions (SBM Report, 2020). SBM's focus on waste management and sanitation behavior has contributed to improved sanitation outcomes, but the issue of water scarcity has complicated its full impact, especially in arid regions like Rajasthan.

2. **National Rural Drinking Water Programme (NRDWP):** The National Rural Drinking Water Programme (NRDWP) is a national initiative aimed at ensuring adequate and safe drinking water in rural areas. Rajasthan has benefited from the program's funding for the installation of piped water supply schemes and the improvement of water quality monitoring mechanisms. The scheme addresses both access to drinking water and water quality issues, crucial for Rajasthan's water-challenged regions (Department of Drinking Water and Sanitation, 2021).

3. **Jal Jeevan Mission (JJM):** Launched in 2019, the Jal Jeevan Mission (JJM) focuses on providing piped water connections to every rural household by 2024. Rajasthan has made progress under JJM, targeting the establishment of robust water supply infrastructure to address the state's water scarcity. The program has a strong focus on water quality, sustainability, and community involvement, with an emphasis on local water management (Jal Jeevan Mission, 2020).

4. **Atal Mission for Rejuvenation and Urban Transformation (AMRUT):** The AMRUT Mission, though primarily for urban areas, has seen implementation in Rajasthan's cities to improve water supply, sewerage systems, and urban sanitation. The mission aims to provide universal coverage of water supply and waste management in urban regions. The focus on enhancing urban water and sanitation infrastructure is crucial, as Rajasthan's cities, like Jaipur and Udaipur, face growing demands due to urbanization (AMRUT Mission, 2021).

**State Policies and Initiatives**

1. Rajasthan Water Sector Restructuring Project (RWSRP): The Rajasthan Water Sector Restructuring Project (RWSRP) is a major state-level initiative aimed at improving water supply, irrigation, and groundwater management in Rajasthan. It has focused on enhancing water-use efficiency and promoting rainwater harvesting, which is essential in a water-scarce state. The project has had positive impacts on improving water availability for both agricultural and domestic use, especially in rural areas (Rajasthan Water Sector Restructuring Project, 2020).

2. State Water Policy (2010): Rajasthan's State Water Policy emphasizes sustainable water management, efficient use of water resources, and conservation practices. The policy focuses on measures to recharge groundwater, increase storage capacity, and improve water distribution networks. While the policy has set ambitious goals for improving water use efficiency, its implementation at the ground level faces challenges such as inadequate infrastructure and funding gaps (Rajasthan State Water Policy, 2010).

3. Rajasthan Rural Water Supply and Sanitation (RWSS) Project: This state project aims to provide clean water and sanitation facilities in rural Rajasthan. It focuses on infrastructure development, particularly in underserved and remote regions. The RWSS initiative integrates health education and behavior change into its programs to promote better sanitation practices, especially in areas with a high prevalence of open defecation (Department of Drinking Water and Sanitation, 2021).

4. Rajasthan State Action Plan on Climate Change (SAPCC): The Rajasthan State Action Plan on Climate Change (SAPCC) includes water resource management

as a critical component, with strategies to address the impacts of climate change on water availability and quality. The plan focuses on enhancing resilience to droughts and floods, promoting water conservation practices, and improving the sustainability of water systems across the state (Rajasthan State Action Plan on Climate Change, 2020).

## *Community Initiatives*

1. **Community-Based Water Management in Jodhpur District:** In Jodhpur, a community-based water management model has been successfully implemented in several villages. The model includes the active involvement of local communities in water harvesting, management, and maintenance of water systems. Through training and awareness campaigns, the community has significantly reduced the dependency on groundwater, switching to surface water harvesting techniques. This model emphasizes decentralized water management and has been recognized as a best practice in Rajasthan (Water Resource Management, Jodhpur, 2019).

2. **Jal Dhara Yojana (Water Pipeline Scheme):** The Jal Dhara Yojana is a Rajasthan government initiative that aims to supply piped water to rural households. In some districts like Alwar and Banswara, this scheme has significantly improved the reliability and quality of water supplied to rural households. Local communities

have been engaged in the operation and maintenance of water infrastructure, leading to better service delivery and sustainable water management practices (Jal Dhara Yojana, 2020).

3. **Rainwater Harvesting in the Thar Desert:** In the arid regions of the Thar Desert, rainwater harvesting has been adapted as a traditional water management practice. Local communities, supported by government schemes and NGOs, have revitalized this practice to ensure a steady water supply during the dry months. The use of check dams, ponds, and johads (traditional water storage structures) has proven effective in conserving water and replenishing groundwater levels (Rajasthan State Water Policy, 2010).

4. **Narmada Water Transfer Project:** The Narmada Water Transfer Project is an ambitious initiative to bring water from the Narmada River to Rajasthan through a series of pipelines and canals. This project aims to provide drinking water to regions suffering from water scarcity, particularly in the southern and eastern parts of the state. Though still in progress, it holds promise for transforming water access in these arid areas (Narmada Water Transfer Project, 2021).

### Gender and Social Inclusion Aspects

The provision of clean water and sanitation has a profound impact on gender equality and social inclusion in Rajasthan. Women and girls, particularly in rural areas, bear the brunt of water collection, often walking long distances to fetch water. Lack of sanitation facilities exacerbates gender disparities, as women face increased health risks and insecurity, particularly during menstruation.

1. **Women's Empowerment:** Several government initiatives aim to empower women through water and sanitation interventions. For instance, the SBM encourages the construction of household toilets, a crucial factor in improving women's health and dignity. However, gender-sensitive interventions are still lacking in water management practices and decision-making processes related to water governance (National Institute of Rural Development, 2020).

2. **Social Inclusion:** Rajasthan's marginalized communities, including Scheduled Castes (SCs), Scheduled Tribes (STs), and other disadvantaged groups, are disproportionately affected by poor water and sanitation facilities. These communities often live in remote areas where infrastructure development is slow, leading to a lack of access to basic water and sanitation services.

**Economic Impacts**

The economic impacts of poor water and sanitation in Rajasthan are far-reaching. The state's reliance on agriculture, particularly in water-scarce areas, is hampered by inconsistent water availability, leading to low agricultural productivity. Poor sanitation also contributes to higher healthcare costs, with waterborne diseases burdening the state's health system. According to a report by the Ministry of Drinking Water and Sanitation, poor water and sanitation in Rajasthan cost the state approximately ₹9,000 crores annually in terms of healthcare costs, lost productivity, and water-related damages (Ministry of Drinking Water and Sanitation, 2021).

**Climate Change Impacts**

Rajasthan's vulnerability to climate change further complicates water and sanitation issues. The state experiences extreme weather conditions, including droughts, high temperatures, and erratic rainfall, which significantly impact water availability. The decreasing groundwater levels, especially in rural and desert regions, are exacerbated by climate change, leading to frequent water shortages (Ministry of Environment, Forests and Climate Change, 2020).

The state's infrastructure, particularly in rural areas, is not sufficiently resilient to climate-induced disruptions, making it difficult to provide consistent access to safe drinking water and sanitation services. Climate adaptation strategies, therefore, need to be integrated into water governance policies in Rajasthan to ensure long-term sustainability.

## *Challenges*

1. **Water Scarcity:** The recurring water scarcity in Rajasthan, exacerbated by high evaporation rates and poor water retention, hampers access to drinking water. Groundwater depletion due to over-extraction for agriculture further limits the availability of potable water (Department of Drinking Water and Sanitation, 2021).

2. **Infrastructure Deficits:** While Rajasthan has made strides in improving water and sanitation infrastructure, many areas still lack reliable and sustainable systems for water distribution and wastewater management (Rajasthan Water Sector Restructuring Project, 2020).

3. **Social Inequality:** Marginalized communities, particularly in rural and tribal areas, continue to face barriers to accessing clean water and sanitation facilities due to social exclusion and discrimination (NITI Aayog, 2020)

## *Recommendations*

1. **Enhanced Water Management:** Rajasthan needs to focus on sustainable water management practices, including rainwater harvesting, groundwater recharge, and improved irrigation efficiency, to cope with water scarcity (Rajasthan State Government Report, 2020).
2. **Focus on Equity:** Government policies must prioritize equity, ensuring that marginalized communities, particularly women, STs, and SCs, benefit from improved water and sanitation services. Gender-sensitive interventions in water management and sanitation design can reduce the burden on women and girls (National Institute of Rural Development, 2020).
3. **Climate-Resilient Infrastructure:** Water and sanitation infrastructure in Rajasthan must be made climate-resilient by incorporating adaptive technologies and practices that can withstand the impacts of climate change (Ministry of Environment, Forests and Climate Change, 2020).
4. **Community Participation:** Greater involvement of local communities in decision-making processes related to water management and sanitation can enhance the sustainability of interventions and ensure that the needs of all segments of society are met (SBM Report, 2020).

## *Best Practices*

1. Goa: Community-Based Water Management

Goa has implemented robust community-driven water resource management initiatives. The "Spring Protection and Recharge Project" ensures the conservation of natural springs, a vital water source in rural and semi-urban areas. The program promotes community participation in identifying and rejuvenating water sources, supported by technical assistance and funding from the state government. Goa's success highlights the importance of integrating traditional water conservation practices with modern technologies (SDG India Index 2023-24).

2. Andaman and Nicobar Islands: Rainwater Harvesting Systems

Given its geographical constraints, the Andaman and Nicobar Islands have adopted rainwater harvesting as a primary water conservation strategy. The islands mandate rooftop rainwater harvesting for all new constructions. Additionally, community rainwater harvesting tanks have been installed in remote areas to ensure year-round water availability. This practice emphasizes the effective utilization of local resources to address water scarcity (Ministry of Jal Shakti, 2023).

3. Kerala: Total Sanitation Campaign

Kerala's "Total Sanitation Campaign", now integrated with the Swachh Bharat Mission, achieved significant success in making the state open defecation-free by 2016. The campaign focused on behavioral change, providing financial incentives for constructing household toilets and engaging local self-government institutions. Kerala's use of awareness campaigns and participatory governance offers valuable lessons in achieving universal sanitation (NITI Aayog, 2023).

4. Sikkim: Sustainable Wastewater Management

Sikkim's efforts in sustainable wastewater treatment through the Integrated Sewerage and Septage Management Program have set benchmarks for other states. The program ensures proper sewage treatment and reuse, reducing environmental contamination and improving sanitation outcomes. Sikkim's approach underscores the importance of integrating environmental sustainability with sanitation strategies (MOSPI, 2023).

5. Maharashtra: Jalyukt Shivar Abhiyan

The Jalyukt Shivar Abhiyan in Maharashtra aims to make villages drought-free by developing water storage and recharge systems. Measures such as desilting ponds, creating farm ponds, and constructing check dams have significantly improved groundwater levels in drought-prone areas. This program is particularly relevant for states like Rajasthan, where water scarcity is a persistent challenge (RBI Reports, 2023).

6. Nagaland: Community-Led Sanitation Programs

Nagaland emphasizes the community-led approach to improve sanitation and hygiene practices. Local councils are empowered to oversee sanitation programs, ensuring the active participation of all households. These decentralized efforts, coupled with awareness campaigns, have improved hygiene standards and reduced waterborne diseases in the region (NFHS 2019-21).

7. Puducherry: Effective Urban Wastewater Management

Puducherry has demonstrated excellence in urban wastewater management through its decentralized treatment plants. The treated water is reused for gardening and other non-potable purposes, conserving freshwater resources. Puducherry's focus on urban sanitation infrastructure provides valuable insights for managing growing urban populations (NITI Aayog, 2023).

## *Conclusion*

Rajasthan's progress in achieving SDG 6 – Clean Water and Sanitation, is constrained by several geographical, infrastructural, and social challenges. While the state has implemented several national and state policies, including the Jal Jeevan Mission, Swachh Bharat Mission, and Rajasthan Water Sector Restructuring Project, issues such as water scarcity, unequal access to water, and social exclusion persist.

Community-driven initiatives, such as rainwater harvesting in the Thar Desert and the Jal Dhara Yojana, offer promising models that could be scaled up. However, sustained efforts, stronger policy implementation, and increased community participation are essential to overcoming Rajasthan's water and sanitation challenges and meeting the targets of SDG 6. Addressing issues such as water scarcity, social inclusion, and the economic impacts of poor water and sanitation will require a multi-faceted approach, integrating infrastructure development, policy reforms, and community engagement. By focusing on sustainability and equity, Rajasthan can improve water and sanitation services, ultimately contributing to the state's overall development and the achievement of SDG 6.

# SDG 7 - Affordable and Clean Energy: A Case Study of Nagaland and Meghalaya

Sustainable Development Goal 7 (SDG 7) envisions universal access to affordable, reliable, and sustainable energy, which is essential for eradicating poverty, fostering economic growth, and combating climate change. Nagaland and Meghalaya, two northeastern states of India, face distinct challenges due to their geographical isolation, rugged terrains, and limited infrastructure. Despite these challenges, both states have made strides in expanding energy access and integrating renewable energy sources into their energy mix. This chapter evaluates their progress using key indicators, analyzes the impact of national and state-specific policies, and provides recommendations for achieving SDG 7 goals.

## *Key Indicators of Affordable and Clean Energy*

### 1. Access to Electricity

Electricity access in Nagaland and Meghalaya has significantly improved in recent years, primarily due to the efforts under the Deen Dayal Upadhyaya Gram Jyoti Yojana (DDU-GJY) and the Saubhagya Scheme. According to the Saubhagya Dashboard (2023), over 95.6% of households in Nagaland have been electrified. However, several remote villages face challenges such as unreliable power supply and frequent outages due to outdated grid infrastructure. Electrification levels in Meghalaya have reached 97.8% as per the NITI Aayog SDG India Index 2023. The state has prioritized connecting hard-to-reach areas, but power reliability remains a concern, especially in rural regions prone to harsh weather conditions.

### 2. Renewable Energy Contribution

Renewable energy plays an increasingly vital role in the energy strategies of both states. Hydropower constitutes the majority of Nagaland's renewable energy production, with projects like the Doyang Hydro Project (75 MW capacity). However, solar energy adoption remains minimal despite the state's potential for solar installations (MNRE, 2023). Approximately 22% of Meghalaya's energy mix is sourced from renewable energy, primarily hydropower. Under the Rooftop Solar Programme, efforts to increase solar energy adoption have been initiated, but the uptake remains slow due to high upfront costs (MOSPI, 2023).

### 3. Access to Clean Cooking Fuel

The use of clean cooking fuel is a critical indicator of energy sustainability. In Nagaland, the Pradhan Mantri Ujjwala Yojana (PMUY) has provided LPG connections to over 75,000 households, increasing the use of clean cooking fuel in rural areas to 45%. However, firewood remains the primary cooking fuel for nearly 55% of households, reflecting the need for behavioral change and affordability improvements (NFHS-5, 2019-21). LPG usage in rural Meghalaya has risen to approximately 60%, supported by PMUY and additional state-level subsidies. Nevertheless, the refill costs of LPG cylinders pose a significant barrier to sustained adoption (NFHS-5, 2019-21).

### 4. Energy Infrastructure

The geographical challenges of Nagaland and Meghalaya hinder the expansion of conventional energy grids. Efforts to improve energy access include decentralized solutions such as solar mini-grids and micro-hydropower projects. Despite these interventions, energy distribution remains inconsistent, especially during the monsoon season (MOSPI, 2023).

# *National and State Policies*

## 1. National Policies and Schemes

Several central government initiatives have significantly influenced energy access and sustainability in Nagaland and Meghalaya:

1. **Deen Dayal Upadhyaya Gram Jyoti Yojana (DDU-GJY):** This scheme has improved rural electrification and separated agricultural and non-agricultural feeders, leading to more efficient energy distribution in both states (RBI Reports, 2023).
2. **Pradhan Mantri Ujjwala Yojana (PMUY):** By subsidizing LPG connections for low-income households, PMUY has played a crucial role in reducing the reliance on biomass fuels in both states.
3. **UJALA Scheme:** The distribution of over 3.5 million LED bulbs in Meghalaya has reduced annual electricity consumption by approximately 300 million kWh (MNRE, 2023).
4. **National Green Hydrogen Mission:** While still in the initial stages, this mission has the potential to support clean energy transition efforts in the northeastern states, particularly for industrial applications.

## 2. State-Specific Policies

1. **The Nagaland Renewable Energy Policy (2016)** focuses on promoting small hydro and solar energy projects, aiming to add 50 MW of renewable capacity by 2030 (NITI Aayog, 2023).

2. **The Meghalaya Energy Conservation Policy (2020)** emphasizes energy efficiency through public awareness campaigns and renewable energy integration.

## Community Initiatives and Local Innovations

Solar-powered microgrids in Nagaland have been installed in remote villages, providing reliable electricity to underserved communities. Also, the community-driven biogas plants in Nagaland offer a sustainable alternative to firewood for cooking, promoting clean energy use at the grassroots level. Women's self-help groups (SHGs) in Meghalaya are being trained in solar panel installation and maintenance, creating employment opportunities while enhancing energy access. Locally managed hydropower plants in Meghalaya ensure sustainable energy generation and equitable distribution within communities.

**Challenges and Constraints**

1. **Geographical Isolation:** The rugged terrain complicates grid expansion and energy distribution in both states.
2. **High Initial Costs:** Renewable energy solutions such as solar installations face financial barriers, limiting widespread adoption.
3. **Cultural Resistance:** Traditional reliance on biomass fuels persists in rural areas, highlighting the need for behavioral interventions.

## Recommendations and Best Practices

Kerala's emphasis on energy-efficient appliances through subsidies and public campaigns offers a replicable model for reducing energy consumption in Nagaland and Meghalaya. The development of large-scale solar parks in Gujarat can inspire similar initiatives in Nagaland's open and hilly terrains. The Andaman and Nicobar Islands' decentralized renewable energy systems provide valuable lessons for off-grid energy access in remote northeastern villages. Wind energy projects in Tamil Nadu highlight the feasibility of small wind turbines in Meghalaya's high-altitude regions.

## Conclusion

Nagaland and Meghalaya have made commendable progress toward achieving SDG 7, driven by central schemes, state policies, and community initiatives. However, the states face persistent challenges such as high costs, infrastructure gaps, and cultural barriers. Adopting best practices from other Indian states, coupled with a focus on behavioral change and innovative financing mechanisms, can accelerate their transition to affordable and clean energy for all.

# CHAPTER EIGHT

# SDG 8 - Decent Work and Economic Growth: A Case Study of Delhi

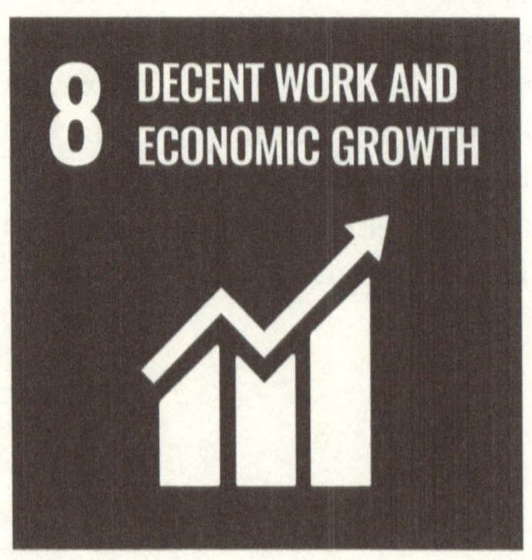


The Sustainable Development Goal (SDG) 8 seeks to promote sustained, inclusive, and sustainable economic growth, full and productive employment, and decent work for all. As India's capital and a major economic hub, Delhi has unique opportunities and challenges in achieving this goal. This chapter examines Delhi's progress toward SDG 8, focusing on indicators, key policies, economic trends, and challenges, with an emphasis on social and economic impacts, migration dynamics, and policy recommendations.

## *Key Indicators and Current Status*

Delhi's performance on SDG 8 can be assessed through indicators like GDP growth, labor force participation, unemployment rates, and job quality. According to the India SDG Index 2023, Delhi scores moderately on SDG 8 indicators but faces significant disparities in job quality and inclusivity (NITI Aayog, 2023). The Periodic Labour Force Survey (PLFS) 2022-23 highlights Delhi's unemployment rate as 6.3%, higher than the national average of 4.1%. However, Delhi's labor force participation rate (LFPR) remains low, especially among women, at just 12.8% (Ministry of Labour and Employment, 2023).

**Economic Growth and Labor Market Trends**

Delhi's Gross State Domestic Product (GSDP) consistently ranks among the highest in India, reaching ₹9.23 lakh crore in 2023-24, driven by its service-dominated economy (RBI, 2023). The city-state contributes approximately 3.8% to India's total GDP, with the finance, real estate, IT, and communications sectors being key drivers. However, the informal sector, employing around 62% of Delhi's workforce, remains a significant yet precarious contributor (World Bank, 2023).

## Employment Patterns and Sectoral Insights

1. **Formal Sector Dominance in Services:** The finance, IT, and public administration sectors offer formal employment opportunities, benefiting from higher wages and social security coverage.
2. **Informal Sector Prevalence:** Construction, domestic work, and street vending dominate Delhi's informal labor market, where workers lack job security, fair wages, and basic entitlements (PLFS, 2023).
3. **Youth Employment Trends:** Delhi's educated youth increasingly enter startups and emerging industries such as e-commerce, supported by initiatives like Startup India. Yet, unemployment among graduates remains disproportionately high at 17% (NITI Aayog, 2023).

### Migration and Urbanization

Delhi's status as a migration magnet shapes its labor dynamics. Nearly 40% of Delhi's population comprises migrants, primarily from Uttar Pradesh, Bihar, and Rajasthan, who contribute significantly to the informal economy (World Bank, 2023). This influx bolsters labor supply but exacerbates urban challenges, including overcrowding, housing shortages, and strained civic infrastructure.

## *Current Policies and Initiatives*

Delhi has implemented several national and state-level policies to boost decent work and economic growth.

Prominent initiatives include:
**National Policies and Their Impact on Delhi**

1. **Make in India:** This initiative seeks to foster innovation, enhance skill development, and encourage investments in manufacturing. While Delhi is not a manufacturing hub, policies under "Make in India" have positively influenced its ancillary sectors, such as logistics and e-commerce. Small and medium enterprises (SMEs) in these sectors have benefited from subsidies and infrastructure support (Ministry of Commerce and Industry, 2023).Small-scale manufacturing and associated employment in the city's industrial clusters, such as Okhla and Bawana, reflect this initiative's regional impact (NITI Aayog, 2023).

2. **Startup India:** Delhi's robust startup ecosystem, supported by financial incentives and incubation centers, has become a hub for fintech, e-commerce, and health tech innovations. In 2023, Delhi accounted for 21% of India's recognized startups (Startup India, 2024).The initiative has led to the establishment of incubation hubs like the Delhi Technology Business Incubator. These hubs provide financial assistance, mentorship, and networking opportunities for young entrepreneurs, addressing the need for decent work through new job creation (Startup India, 2024).

3. **Skill India Mission:** Through targeted programs like the Delhi Skill Development Mission (DSDM), the national focus on skills has been localized. Training programs in high-demand sectors, including IT, healthcare, and retail, have increased employability. DSDM has trained over 600,000 individuals in Delhi since its inception, significantly contributing to SDG 8 targets (Skill

Development India, 2024).

4.  **E-Shram Portal:** Delhi has registered over 1.5 million informal workers on the national e-Shram portal. This registration ensures these workers are eligible for social security schemes, health benefits, and financial inclusion, addressing some of the vulnerabilities associated with informal employment (Ministry of Labour and Employment, 2023).

5.  **Digital India:** Delhi has been a leader in implementing Digital India initiatives, particularly in promoting digital payments and e-governance. This has created new forms of employment in the gig economy and enhanced productivity across industries (MeitY, 2023).

6.  **Targeted Public Distribution System (TPDS):** Delhi's Aadhaar-enabled TPDS ensures food security for vulnerable groups. This indirectly supports SDG 8 by allowing economically disadvantaged populations to channel saved resources toward education, skill development, and employment (NITI Aayog, 2023).

**State Policies**

1.  **Delhi Employment Guarantee Scheme:** Modeled on the National Rural Employment Guarantee Scheme (NREGS), this program offers urban job seekers guaranteed work in community development projects, primarily in unauthorized colonies and resettlement areas.

2.  **Urban Livelihood Mission:** Implemented in partnership with the central government, the National Urban Livelihood Mission (NULM) in Delhi focuses on improving livelihoods in slums. It has enabled the formation of self-help groups and provided access to

skill training and micro-financing for small businesses (World Bank, 2023).

3. **Delhi Skill Development Corporation (DSDC):** This corporation offers industry-specific certifications and placements. Programs such as mobile repair, computer programming, and hospitality training have significantly bridged skill gaps in the workforce.

## *Community Initiatives*

1. **Self-Help Groups (SHGs):** In low-income areas of Delhi, women-led SHGs have demonstrated resilience by establishing small-scale businesses, such as tailoring units and catering services. These groups benefit from micro-loans provided under NULM and local cooperative banks (ILO, 2023).
2. **Street Vendor Rehabilitation:** Delhi's Municipal Corporation has created designated zones for street vendors, ensuring they have access to safe vending spaces and financial inclusion through vendor cards. The Street Vendors (Protection of Livelihood and Regulation of Street Vending) Act, 2014, has been instrumental in supporting this initiative (Ministry of Labour, 2023).
3. **Green Economy Initiatives:** The Delhi government has piloted several projects integrating decent work and environmental sustainability. Programs such as solar panel installations on public buildings and waste management ventures provide green jobs while addressing climate change (Delhi Government, 2023).

4. **Gig Economy Interventions:** Platforms like UrbanClap and Swiggy have transformed Delhi's job landscape by creating flexible employment opportunities. While these platforms provide additional income, ensuring fair pay and social security for gig workers remains a challenge (ILO, 2023).

5. **Incubation and Mentorship Models:** Delhi-based incubation centers, such as the IIT Delhi Incubator, offer structured mentorship, financial support, and industry collaboration opportunities for startups. These centers enhance job creation while fostering innovation (Startup India, 2024).

6. **Skill-Employer Linkage:** Collaborations between Delhi's skill centers and industries ensure job-ready candidates. A pilot program connecting hospitality trainees with prominent hotels resulted in 85% placement rates (Skill Development India, 2024).

7. **Urban Informal Sector Empowerment:** NGOs like SEWA Delhi empower informal workers, particularly women, by advocating for their rights, organizing skill training, and ensuring their access to basic services (SEWA, 2024).

## *Challenges*

1. **Informal Sector Predominance:** The informal sector in Delhi remains a major employer but lacks job security, benefits, and adequate wages. Workers in this sector face exploitation and limited upward mobility (ILO, 2023).

2. **Gender Disparities:** Women's participation in Delhi's workforce is among the lowest in India, attributed to socio-cultural barriers, inadequate childcare facilities, and lack of safe transportation (PLFS, 2023).

3. **Migration Pressures:** Delhi attracts a large migrant population seeking employment. This influx often leads to overcrowded living conditions, exploitation of migrant workers, and strain on urban infrastructure (World Bank, 2023).

4. **Environmental Constraints:** Air pollution and water scarcity in Delhi deter business investments and affect worker productivity, posing indirect challenges to economic growth (Ministry of Environment, Forest and Climate Change, 2023).

5. **Automation and Job Displacement:** The rise of automation and digitalization in industries like retail and manufacturing has led to job displacement, particularly for low-skilled workers (World Economic Forum, 2023).

6. **Social and Economic Impacts:** Despite economic growth, income inequality persists in Delhi, with a significant gap between formal and informal sector wages (RBI, 2023). The lack of decent work opportunities in low-income neighborhoods exacerbates urban poverty. Delhi's educated youth face high unemployment rates due to a mismatch between skills and job market demands (Skill Development India, 2024).

## *Recommendations*

1. **Strengthening the Informal Sector:** Policies should focus on formalizing the informal sector by providing financial incentives, social security, and skill development programs tailored to this workforce.
2. **Promoting Women's Participation:** Addressing gender disparities through initiatives like workplace childcare facilities, safer public transport, and targeted skill development for women can boost workforce inclusion.
3. **Encouraging Green Jobs:** Investments in renewable energy and green infrastructure can create sustainable job opportunities while addressing environmental concerns.
4. **Enhanced Urban Planning:** Developing affordable housing and improving urban infrastructure can mitigate the challenges of migration and overcrowding.
5. **Fostering Digital Inclusion:** Expanding digital literacy programs and providing affordable internet access can empower workers and small businesses to thrive in a digital economy.

## Best Practices from Other States and UTs

Karnataka has emerged as a leader in promoting the micro, small, and medium enterprises (MSME) sector by leveraging technology. The e-Udyami Portal, launched by the state government, provides a digital platform for MSMEs to access information on government schemes, financing options, and marketing support. Initiatives like the Bengaluru Tech Summit and partnerships with private stakeholders have driven innovation and employment in the technology sector. With its burgeoning startup ecosystem, Delhi can implement a similar digital platform for MSMEs, ensuring access to resources for small-scale entrepreneurs. Emulating Karnataka's focus on innovation could further strengthen Delhi's position as a hub for technology-driven industries.

Himachal Pradesh has effectively combined skill development with tourism promotion. The Skill Development Allowance Scheme provides financial assistance for vocational training, enabling youth to find employment in the tourism and hospitality sectors. Programs like Har Gaon Ki Kahani promote rural tourism, creating jobs in remote areas while preserving cultural heritage. As a global tourist destination, Delhi can benefit by replicating Himachal Pradesh's model to train its workforce in hospitality management and heritage tourism, leveraging its cultural landmarks and diverse cuisine.

Telangana's focus on inclusive economic growth has set benchmarks in rural employment and industrial development. The TS-iPASS (Telangana State Industrial Project Approval and Self-Certification System) simplifies the process of setting up industries, attracting investments, and creating jobs. The Rythu Bandhu Scheme, providing financial support to farmers, has indirectly boosted rural employment by increasing agricultural productivity and demand for allied services. Adopting a streamlined industrial policy similar to TS-iPASS could attract investments in Delhi's peri-urban areas. Additionally, schemes encouraging entrepreneurship in allied agricultural services could address gaps in the informal labor market.

Kerala's Aawaz Health Insurance Scheme ensures access to free healthcare for interstate migrant workers, enhancing their working conditions. Additionally, the Apna Ghar Housing Scheme provides affordable accommodation for migrants, reducing vulnerability. With a large population of migrant workers, Delhi can draw from Kerala's experience to improve housing and healthcare facilities, ensuring decent work environments.

Gujarat's Mission Mangalam program supports women's self-help groups (SHGs) through skill training, financial literacy, and credit linkages, enabling them to become entrepreneurs. Given its urbanized setting, a similar initiative in Delhi could empower women in slum and resettlement areas, fostering economic independence and closing the gender wage gap.

## Conclusion

Delhi's progress toward SDG 8 reflects its potential as an economic powerhouse. However, achieving inclusive and sustainable economic growth requires a multi-faceted approach that addresses the challenges of informality, inequality, and gender disparities. Strengthening community participation, leveraging technology, and promoting policy innovation will be crucial in realizing decent work and economic growth for all in Delhi.

# CHAPTER NINE

# SDG 9 – Industry, Innovation and Infrastructure: A Case Study on Arunachal Pradesh and Tripura

Sustainable Development Goal 9 (SDG 9) emphasizes the development of resilient infrastructure, inclusive industrialization, and innovation as essential drivers for sustainable growth. Arunachal Pradesh and Tripura, two northeastern states of India, hold unique potential and face distinct challenges in advancing these goals. Their geographical isolation, socio-economic constraints, and infrastructural deficits are balanced by rich natural resources, cultural diversity, and opportunities offered through national and international initiatives like the Act East Policy.

## Key Indicators

### Industrial Development

Arunachal Pradesh primarily supports micro and small-scale industries, with sectors like horticulture, forest-based crafts, and local textiles being significant contributors. The state's industrial contribution to GDP remains low, reflecting untapped potential (RBI, State Finances Report 2024). Tripura has advanced rubber production, tea cultivation, and bamboo-based industries, accounting for a growing share of the state's economy. Tripura's strategic location near Bangladesh offers significant export potential (Ministry of Commerce and Industry, 2024).

### Infrastructure

The Trans-Arunachal Highway, critical for internal connectivity, is progressing but faces delays due to land acquisition challenges. Hydropower projects, including the Subansiri Lower Dam, highlight the state's renewable energy potential (Ministry of Transport, Annual Infrastructure Development Report 2024). The Agartala-

Akhaura rail link enhances trade and people-to-people connections with Bangladesh. Improved road networks under the Pradhan Mantri Gram Sadak Yojana (PMGSY) have reduced rural isolation (Ministry of Rural Development, 2023).

### Innovation

Limited research and development (R&D) infrastructure in both states impedes industrial and technological growth. Programs like the Atal Innovation Mission (AIM) aim to foster grassroots innovation by setting up tinkering labs and incubation centers (NITI Aayog, 2023).

### Energy Access

Arunachal Pradesh's hydropower capacity is substantial, but projects often face delays due to environmental and social concerns. Tripura's focus on solar energy has provided decentralized solutions for rural households (Ministry of Power, 2024).

## *National Policies and Initiatives*

The Indian government has implemented several policies to enhance industrialization and infrastructure while promoting innovation in the northeastern region.

1. **Make in India:** The Make in India initiative has provided a robust framework to promote domestic manufacturing. Arunachal Pradesh has leveraged this program to focus on industries aligned with its natural resources, such as bamboo, timber, and medicinal plants. Tripura, with its rubber and tea industries, has seen increased investments, particularly in agro-processing and eco-tourism (Ministry of Commerce and

Industry, 2024). The initiative has also encouraged private players to invest in small-scale industries, leading to job creation and the development of local markets.

2. **Ease of Doing Business (EoDB):** Simplified regulations under the Ease of Doing Business initiative have significantly benefited Tripura and Arunachal Pradesh. Tripura's implementation of a single-window clearance system has streamlined industrial approval processes, while Arunachal Pradesh offers fiscal incentives to attract investors (DPIIT, 2024). These measures have improved business confidence, fostering a conducive environment for industrial growth.

3. **Special Accelerated Road Development Programme in the Northeast (SARDP-NE):** Recognizing the need for better connectivity, the SARDP-NE aims to develop an extensive road network connecting northeastern states to national highways. Projects like the Trans-Arunachal Highway and improvements in Tripura's road infrastructure have enhanced trade and mobility (Ministry of Transport, 2024). These developments have facilitated the transport of goods and services, boosting local economies.

4. **Atal Innovation Mission (AIM):** The Atal Innovation Mission has been instrumental in fostering grassroots innovation. Over 50 tinkering labs in Tripura and several in Arunachal Pradesh nurture innovation among youth (NITI Aayog, 2023). Through the establishment of tinkering labs and incubation centers, both states have focused on promoting entrepreneurial ventures in renewable energy, agriculture, and information technology.

5. **MGNREGA (Mahatma Gandhi National Rural Employment Guarantee Act):** MGNREGA has played a pivotal role in building rural infrastructure, such as irrigation systems, roads, and small-scale dams. This infrastructure has supported industrial activities in remote areas of Arunachal Pradesh and Tripura, providing a foundation for sustainable development (Ministry of Rural Development, 2023).

6. **North East Industrial Development Scheme (NEIDS):** The NEIDS has provided financial incentives to industries in the region, encouraging investments in sectors like textiles, food processing, and renewable energy. The scheme has created job opportunities and fostered economic growth in both states.

**State Policies and Programs**

Both Arunachal Pradesh and Tripura have tailored policies to complement national initiatives while addressing regional challenges. Arunachal Pradesh's industrial policy 2022 emphasizes eco-friendly industries and small-scale manufacturing. Tax holidays and exemptions for small businesses have attracted investments in bamboo-based industries, medicinal plants, and handicrafts (Government of Arunachal Pradesh, 2022). The Tripura Bamboo Mission has revitalized bamboo industries by offering R&D support and technical training. This mission has significantly contributed to export growth and the establishment of bamboo-based enterprises (Government of Tripura, 2024). The state of Arunachal Pradesh has focused on renewable energy projects like the Subansiri Lower Dam to cater to industrial and domestic energy needs. In the case of Tripura, cross-border trade initiatives, such as the Agartala-Akhaura rail link with

Bangladesh, have facilitated market access for local products.

**Community Initiatives and Best Models**

Local self-help groups (SHGs) in Arunachal Pradesh produce handicrafts and agro-products, such as honey and medicinal plants. These SHGs have gained support through partnerships with NGOs and state government programs. In Tripura, rubber cooperatives have adopted sustainable practices, enhancing productivity and environmental sustainability. Tripura Solar Park, a community-driven initiative supplies clean energy to off-grid villages, reducing dependence on conventional sources (Ministry of New and Renewable Energy, 2023).Small-scale hydropower projects in Arunachal Pradesh have been successfully managed by local communities, providing electricity to remote areas. Innovation hubs established under Atal Innovation Mission have focused on promoting entrepreneurship among youth. These centers have driven innovations in agriculture and renewable energy, particularly in Tripura and Arunachal Pradesh.

## *Challenges*

**Geographical and Infrastructural Constraints**

Arunachal Pradesh's rugged terrain and limited road and rail networks hinder industrial growth and connectivity. In Tripura, despite recent infrastructure developments, logistical bottlenecks and dependency on neighboring states persist.

**Socio-Economic Barriers**

Tribal land ownership in Arunachal Pradesh complicates land acquisition for industrial projects. Similar issues arise in Tripura, where community lands are protected under local laws (World Bank, Sustainable Infrastructure Report 2024). High poverty levels and skill gaps limit the local workforce's employability in emerging industries.

### Environmental Concerns

Large-scale hydroelectric projects in Arunachal Pradesh risk biodiversity loss and displacement of local communities. Rubber plantations in Tripura have raised questions about monoculture's ecological impact (Ministry of Environment, Forest and Climate Change, 2024).

### Social and Economic Impacts

Initiatives under MGNREGA and self-help groups (SHGs) in both states have empowered marginalized communities, especially women, by providing employment and entrepreneurial opportunities (Ministry of Rural Development, 2023). The Agartala-Akhaura rail link and Arunachal's hydropower projects are projected to significantly boost regional GDP and cross-border trade (RBI, 2024). Programs promoting women's participation in handicrafts and agro-based industries have enhanced gender equality. Youth skilling initiatives under the Skill India Mission focus on digital literacy and green technologies.

## *Recommendations*

To foster sustainable development in the northeastern states, it is crucial to accelerate the completion of strategic infrastructure projects such as the Trans-Arunachal Highway, SARDP-NE projects, and the Sela Pass Tunnel, while expanding rail connectivity in Tripura to better integrate with Indian and Bangladeshi markets and developing inland waterways to address logistical challenges. Promoting innovation requires establishing R&D centers focusing on regional resources like medicinal plants in Arunachal Pradesh and bamboo in Tripura, along with encouraging public-private partnerships (PPPs) to fund advancements in energy, transport, and industrial sectors. Environmental sustainability must be prioritized by enforcing strict environmental norms for large-scale projects, promoting community-based afforestation, streamlining land acquisition laws while safeguarding tribal rights, and encouraging agroforestry and diversified cropping in Tripura to mitigate the adverse effects of monoculture plantations. Enhancing private investment involves creating industrial zones offering long-term investment guarantees and tax benefits, especially for eco-friendly industries, while skill development programs should be strengthened to emphasize renewable energy technologies and digital skills to prepare the workforce for future demands. Social inclusion is equally vital, requiring support for self-help groups (SHGs) and cooperatives to integrate local communities into industrial value chains, along with increasing women's participation in industrial activities through targeted skill development initiatives.

## *Best Practices from Other States and UTs*

To achieve Sustainable Development Goal 9 (SDG 9), which emphasizes resilient infrastructure, inclusive industrialization, and innovation, states and Union Territories in India have implemented exemplary policies and initiatives. These best practices provide actionable insights for Arunachal Pradesh and Tripura to overcome their developmental challenges. Goa has prioritized the establishment of environmentally sustainable industrial estates through policies that incentivize green technologies and eco-friendly manufacturing. The state has implemented pollution mitigation measures and waste management systems in industrial zones, ensuring minimal environmental impact while boosting economic activities (NITI Aayog, 2023). This model could guide Tripura and Arunachal Pradesh in developing industrial hubs that prioritize sustainability.

Kerala's focus on fostering innovation-driven industries through incubation centers and startup ecosystems is exemplary. Programs like the Kerala Startup Mission (KSUM) offer mentorship, funding, and infrastructure for budding entrepreneurs. Arunachal Pradesh and Tripura could adopt similar initiatives to encourage local innovations, particularly in sectors like bamboo-based products and renewable energy (Economic and Political Weekly, 2022).

Delhi has established a comprehensive urban infrastructure network, including metro connectivity and logistics hubs, enabling seamless transportation and trade. The Delhi-Mumbai Industrial Corridor (DMIC) exemplifies how strategic planning can enhance industrial output and connectivity (SDG India Index, 2023). Tripura, with its proximity to Bangladesh, could replicate such models by developing inland container depots and cross-border trade zones to strengthen economic ties and export potential.

Haryana has implemented schemes such as the Haryana MSME Policy and Cluster Development Programs, which focus on capacity building, credit support, and market linkages for small and medium enterprises. These initiatives are particularly relevant for Arunachal Pradesh and Tripura, where MSMEs can play a pivotal role in employment generation and economic diversification (Ministry of MSME, 2023).

Punjab's success in integrating agro-industries with local farming communities demonstrates how value chains can boost rural economies. The Punjab Agri Export Corporation has linked farmers to global markets, providing better price realization and reducing post-harvest losses. Tripura and Arunachal Pradesh could benefit from replicating this model by promoting agro-processing industries that capitalize on their rich agricultural and horticultural resources (World Bank, 2023).

Himachal Pradesh is a leader in renewable energy generation, with policies that facilitate the development of hydroelectric power projects while maintaining ecological balance. Programs such as Himachal Hydro Development Scheme can guide Arunachal Pradesh in optimizing its untapped hydroelectric potential. Tripura, with its biomass and solar energy prospects, can adopt Himachal's approach to create a reliable and sustainable energy infrastructure (Ministry of Power, 2023).

## Conclusion

Arunachal Pradesh and Tripura exemplify the opportunities and challenges of pursuing SDG 9 in a region characterized by geographical isolation and rich natural resources. Both the states have made significant progress in advancing SDG 9 through a combination of national policies, state initiatives, and community-driven models. By fostering innovation, enhancing infrastructure, and empowering local communities, these states can set benchmarks for balanced and resilient growth in India's northeastern region. Tailored policy interventions, infrastructure investments, and sustainable practices are critical for leveraging their unique strengths while addressing existing barriers.

# CHAPTER TEN

# SDG 10 – Reduced Inequalities: A Case Study on Mizoram and Rajasthan

Reducing inequalities is a fundamental pillar of the United Nations Sustainable Development Goals (SDGs), aimed at addressing economic, social, and regional disparities. In the year 2023-2024, 45.61% seats of Panchayati Raj Institutions are held by women. 28.57% representation of SC/ST persons have been seen in state legislative assemblies.

SDG 10 focuses on fostering inclusion, equity, and justice while reducing disparities in income, opportunities, and access to resources. Mizoram, a predominantly tribal state with high literacy rates but geographical isolation, and Rajasthan, a socio-economically diverse state grappling with entrenched caste and gender disparities, provide contrasting yet insightful case studies on the challenges and progress in achieving SDG 10.

## *Key Indicators*

Evaluating inequalities in Mizoram and Rajasthan involves a nuanced understanding of income distribution, social status, and accessibility to resources and opportunities.

**1. Income Inequality and Gini Coefficient**

Rajasthan has a Gini coefficient of approximately 0.32, reflecting moderate income inequality, exacerbated by urban-rural divides and uneven economic development (NITI Aayog, 2023). Agricultural wage disparities remain significant. Mizoram exhibits relatively lower income inequality due to communal landholding practices and cultural cohesiveness; however, urban centers show widening disparities with growing migration and urbanization (India SDG Index, 2023).

**2. Social Indicators**

1.  **Infant Mortality Rate (IMR):** Rajasthan's IMR stands at 30 per 1,000 live births, far higher than Mizoram's 5, underscoring gaps in healthcare access and quality (Ministry of Health and Family Welfare, 2023).
2.  **Maternal Mortality Rate (MMR):** Rajasthan's MMR of 164 per 100,000 live births is significantly higher than Mizoram's 61, reflecting disparities in maternal care services (MoHFW, 2023).
3.  **Dropout Rates:** Rajasthan faces severe educational disparities, particularly among rural and female students. Mizoram's literacy rate of 91.3% contrasts sharply with its dropout rates, especially at the secondary level (ASER, 2024).

### 3. Human Development Indices

1.  **Human Development Index (HDI):** Rajasthan ranks among the lower-performing states in India on HDI due to deficits in health and education. Mizoram's higher HDI reflects better performance in literacy and life expectancy (UNDP, 2023).
2.  **Inequality-Adjusted HDI (IHDI):** Mizoram shows fewer losses due to inequality compared to Rajasthan, where caste and gender disparities significantly impact development outcomes (India SDG Index, 2023).

## *National Policies and Initiatives*

1.  **Mahatma Gandhi National Rural Employment Guarantee Act (MGNREGA):** MGNREGA provides a safety net for rural populations by guaranteeing 100

days of wage employment annually. Rajasthan, with its extensive rural population, has benefited significantly, ensuring income stability for marginalized communities (NITI Aayog, 2023). Mizoram utilizes MGNREGA to address urban-rural divides and empower tribal communities, particularly in remote regions where traditional employment opportunities are scarce (MoSPI, 2023).

2. **National Food Security Act (NFSA) and Public Distribution System (PDS):** In Rajasthan, e-PDS has improved transparency and efficiency, ensuring food security for vulnerable populations. Mizoram faces logistical challenges due to its difficult terrain, but community-based interventions help mitigate food distribution issues (India SDG Index, 2023).

3. **Pradhan Mantri Awas Yojana (PMAY):** Rajasthan's urban and rural housing programs under PMAY aim to reduce housing inequalities. Mizoram has adopted innovative approaches, such as integrating sustainable materials for housing construction in tribal areas (Ministry of Housing and Urban Affairs, 2023).

4. **Skill India Mission and Make in India:** These programs aim to reduce skill gaps and increase employability. Rajasthan has leveraged these schemes to enhance vocational training for women and marginalized groups. Mizoram focuses on skilling its tribal youth to promote entrepreneurship and local employment opportunities (Ministry of Skill Development and Entrepreneurship, 2023).

5. **Beti Bachao Beti Padhao and Mid-Day Meal Scheme:** Rajasthan emphasizes reducing gender disparities by promoting female education through Beti Bachao Beti Padhao. The Mid-Day Meal Scheme in both states

ensures nutritional security for children, increasing school attendance and retention rates, particularly for girls (MoHFW, 2023).

6. **Integrated Poverty Alleviation Programs:** Programs like the National Social Assistance Programme (NSAP) and National Rural Livelihoods Mission (NRLM) focus on empowering vulnerable groups. Rajasthan's NRLM has successfully created women-led self-help groups (SHGs). Mizoram's New Land Use Policy (NLUP) aims to improve the self-sufficiency of farmers through sustainable agricultural practices (MoSPI, 2023).

**State-Specific Policies**

1. **Rajasthan Rural Livelihood Project (RRLP):** The RRLP strengthens the livelihoods of rural communities by promoting skill development, financial inclusion, and market linkages. This initiative has proven crucial in addressing rural poverty and inequality.

2. **Mizoram State Flagship Program:** The New Economic Development Policy (NEDP) and Mizoram Skill Mission focus on transforming the state into a market-based economy while preserving tribal identities. The Mizoram State Rural Livelihoods Mission (MSRLM) addresses rural poverty by fostering SHGs and enhancing market access.

## *Community Initiatives and Best Models*

In Rajasthan, Saansad Adarsh Gram Yojana (SAGY) promotes model village development through participatory planning. Villages adopting SAGY's principles have shown improvements in education, healthcare, and infrastructure (MoSPI, 2023). Women-led SHGs in Rajasthan's rural areas have improved financial inclusion and entrepreneurial opportunities (UNDP, 2023). Initiatives such as the Bhamashah Yojana promote financial inclusion and women's empowerment through direct benefit transfers (DBTs).

In the case of Mizoram, New Land Use Policy (NLUP) aims to reduce rural poverty and enhance self-sufficiency among farmers by promoting sustainable agricultural practices and providing alternative livelihoods. The North East Rural Livelihood Project (NERLP) focuses on capacity building and skilling of rural communities, ensuring inclusive growth.

## *Challenges*

1. **Economic Inequalities:** Rajasthan experiences significant income disparities between urban and rural areas, with marginalized communities often excluded from economic opportunities. In Mizoram, market isolation and limited industrialization restrict income growth (India SDG Index, 2023).
2. **Social Inequalities:** Rajasthan exhibits one of the lowest female labor force participation rates in India due to socio-cultural constraints. In contrast, Mizoram's matrilineal traditions provide relatively greater social status to women, though disparities still exist in urban job markets (ILO, 2023).
3. **Regional Disparities:** Rajasthan faces stark contrasts in development between its arid western regions and industrial hubs. Mizoram's geographical isolation

hinders equitable access to resources and services (World Bank, 2023). Migration from rural Rajasthan to urban centers has exacerbated rural-urban divides. Mizoram's out-migration for education and employment leads to a brain drain, impacting its developmental potential (NSSO, 2023).

4. **Tax and Industrial Policies:** Rajasthan benefits from GST reforms, but informal workers remain vulnerable. Mizoram's industries are still in nascent stages, requiring policy support to attract private investment (Ministry of Commerce and Industry, 2024).

## *Recommendations*

To drive sustainable development in Mizoram and Rajasthan, policy enhancements should prioritize strengthening tribal-focused schemes in Mizoram to ensure sustainable livelihoods and equitable access to resources, alongside enforcing anti-discrimination laws and promoting gender-sensitive budgeting in Rajasthan. Economic empowerment initiatives should expand microfinance and cooperative models to uplift marginalized groups in both states and develop agro-industrial hubs in rural regions to boost local economies. Infrastructure development efforts must focus on improving connectivity in Mizoram to enhance market access for agricultural produce, while Rajasthan requires investments in irrigation and renewable energy projects to address regional disparities. Social inclusion can be fostered through awareness campaigns in Rajasthan to combat caste and gender biases and by facilitating inter-community exchanges in Mizoram to address tribal marginalization.

## *Best Practices from other States and UTs*

Goa's targeted welfare programs, such as the Dayanand Social Security Scheme, ensure financial support for vulnerable populations, including the elderly, widows, and disabled individuals. The program's efficiency in providing direct financial assistance can be adapted to address similar vulnerabilities in Mizoram and Rajasthan. Goa's focus on universal healthcare schemes further supports equitable access to health services. Himachal Pradesh has excelled in reducing rural-urban inequalities through initiatives like Prakritik Kheti Khushhal Kisan Yojana promoting sustainable and zero-budget natural farming practices. This approach has uplifted small and marginal farmers, improving their livelihoods. Rajasthan and Mizoram can replicate similar programs tailored to local agricultural practices and resources. Sikkim's policies emphasize gender parity and tribal empowerment through reservation policies in education and employment. The state's commitment to gender equality is reflected in its high Gender Parity Index (SDG India Index, 2023-24). Mizoram can learn from these policies to strengthen its tribal welfare schemes, while Rajasthan can adopt gender-focused measures to close its gender gap.

Manipur promotes social inclusion through Self-Help Groups (SHGs) and cooperatives, particularly among women and tribal communities. Programs like the Start-Up Manipur initiative encourage entrepreneurial ventures, enhancing economic self-reliance. Rajasthan and Mizoram can adapt similar models to empower marginalized communities. Punjab's Mai Bhago Vidya Scheme provides free bicycles to girls to reduce dropout rates, especially in rural areas. This initiative improves access to education and bridges gender disparities, a practice that could be extended to both Rajasthan and Mizoram to address educational inequalities. Kerala's robust social protection measures, such as the Kerala Social Security Mission and its social security schemes for widows, the elderly, and persons with disabilities, ensure broad social coverage. Its high literacy rates and decentralized governance model empower marginalized communities and women. Rajasthan and Mizoram can draw from Kerala's inclusive policy frameworks to ensure more equitable social development.Tamil Nadu has implemented several welfare programs targeting marginalized groups, such as the Amma Unavagam (low-cost canteens) and free distribution of essential commodities. The state's focus on gender equality through reservation in local governance and incentives for girl child education serves as a replicable model for addressing inequalities in Mizoram and Rajasthan. Puducherry has implemented comprehensive social security systems and universal access to basic services, including health, education, and subsidized housing. Its efficient service delivery model ensures equitable resource distribution, an approach Mizoram and Rajasthan can emulate to address systemic disparities. Chandigarh's urban planning includes initiatives to integrate low-income groups into mainstream development through public housing schemes and skill development programs. Such practices are crucial for addressing urban inequalities in Rajasthan's expanding cities and Mizoram's growing urban centers.

## *Conclusion*

Achieving SDG 10 in Mizoram and Rajasthan requires a multi-faceted approach that incorporates localized strategies within the broader framework of national policies. Mizoram's social cohesion and high literacy provide a strong foundation, yet geographical and market barriers remain significant. Rajasthan's diverse socio-economic landscape necessitates targeted interventions to address caste and gender inequalities. By prioritizing inclusion, resource equity, and community engagement, these states can move closer to reducing inequalities and fostering sustainable development.

# CHAPTER ELEVEN

# SDG 11 – Sustainable Cities and Communities: A Case Study of Ladakh and North-Eastern States

Sustainable urbanization is fundamental to addressing the social, economic, and environmental challenges of growing cities. SDG 11 emphasizes creating inclusive, resilient, and sustainable human settlements by tackling issues like housing shortages, environmental degradation, urban planning, and disaster resilience. Ladakh and the North Eastern states present unique scenarios due to their geographical isolation, fragile ecosystems, cultural diversity, and socio-economic challenges. Understanding their approaches and limitations in achieving SDG 11 provides insights into how such regions can balance growth with sustainability.

## *Key Indicators*

### Safe and Affordable Housing

Ladakh and the North Eastern states face severe housing shortages exacerbated by natural disasters and geographic constraints. The 2019 National Sample Survey Office (NSSO) report highlights that over 60% of households in these regions rely on temporary structures. Ladakh utilizes traditional materials like mud and stone to build thermally efficient homes, though these are inadequate to meet rising demand. In Assam, recurring floods damage housing infrastructure, leading to annual reconstruction costs (NITI Aayog, 2023).

### Affordable and Sustainable Transport Systems

Connectivity remains a significant barrier in both regions. Ladakh has limited all-weather roads, while the North East suffers from underdeveloped rail and road networks. Initiatives like the Bharatmala Pariyojana and FAME II have improved electric vehicle adoption and road development in cities like Shillong and Gangtok. However, these efforts have yet to achieve wide-scale impact (Ministry of Transport, 2023).

### Inclusive and Sustainable Urbanization

Urbanization in these regions is uneven, with Ladakh experiencing seasonal population surges due to tourism and the North East facing migration-induced urban sprawl. The rise of informal settlements, especially in Guwahati, highlights the need for integrated urban planning to accommodate growth without exacerbating inequalities.

### Pollution and Waste Management

Cities like Leh and Shillong face significant pollution due to inadequate waste disposal systems. According to the Ministry of Housing and Urban Affairs (MoHUA, 2023), solid waste generation has increased by 20% over the past decade in these regions. Shillong has piloted composting initiatives, but systemic gaps in waste segregation persist.

### Water Supply and Green Infrastructure

The fragile ecosystems of Ladakh and the North East face water scarcity due to climate change. In Ladakh, glacier retreat disrupts traditional water sources, while rapid urbanization in Guwahati has led to declining groundwater levels. Projects like Jal Jeevan Mission aim to improve water supply infrastructure, but implementation remains uneven (MoSPI, 2023).

## National and State Policies/Schemes

1. **Pradhan Mantri Awaas Yojana (PMAY):** Both urban and rural components of PMAY have seen significant implementation in these regions. In Ladakh, eco-friendly designs are encouraged under PMAY to address

climatic challenges. The North East integrates traditional bamboo housing with modern techniques to improve disaster resilience (NITI Aayog, 2023).

2. **AMRUT (Atal Mission for Rejuvenation and Urban Transformation):** This scheme focuses on urban infrastructure improvements in water supply and sewerage. While Gangtok and Aizawl have seen measurable progress, cities in Ladakh are yet to be covered comprehensively.

3. **Smart Cities Mission:** Shillong's inclusion in this mission has facilitated projects for smart waste management and IT-based urban services.

4. **National Clean Air Programme (NCAP):** Cities like Shillong are part of NCAP's initiative to reduce particulate matter (PM2.5 and PM10) by 20–30% by 2024. NCAP emphasizes air pollution monitoring, stricter emission norms, and promoting green energy solutions.

5. **Mission Amrut Sarovar:** Focused on rejuvenating urban water bodies, the mission has been piloted in Aizawl and Leh to create resilient water systems.

6. **PM Street Vendor's AtmaNirbhar Nidhi (PM SVANidhi):** Provides financial assistance to street vendors, fostering inclusive urban growth. In Gangtok and Shillong, this program supports the informal economy, with over 12,000 loans disbursed regionally (MoHUA, 2023).

7. **Mahatma Gandhi National Rural Employment Guarantee Act (MGNREGA):** Though primarily rural, MGNREGA is integrated into urban fringe development in areas like Guwahati, where it aids in building infrastructure for informal settlements.

## Community Initiatives

Grassroots organizations in Shillong promote composting and waste segregation, setting an example for other cities. Community-led initiatives supported by the Ladakh Renewable Energy Development Agency (LREDA) integrate solar energy into homes and public buildings. Funded by the Asian Development Bank, North Eastern Region Urban Development Programme (NERUDP) focuses on solid waste management, water supply, and urban transport in select North Eastern cities (NERUDP, 2023).

## Challenges

1. Construction and Urban Planning: Ladakh's reliance on traditional construction methods is unsustainable for modern housing demands, while urban planning in the North East is hindered by weak institutional capacity and unregulated growth.
2. Slums and Informal Settlements: Guwahati has witnessed a rise in slums, home to over 30% of its urban population (India SDG Index, 2023). These areas lack basic amenities, contributing to poor living standards.
3. Environmental Pressures: Waste accumulation in tourist-heavy regions like Leh and uncontrolled vehicular emissions in urban North Eastern cities worsen environmental degradation.
4. Migration and Population Density: Seasonal and permanent migration strains resources in cities like Shillong, leading to overcrowded public services and

infrastructure (Ministry of Statistics and Programme Implementation, 2023).

## *RECOMMENDATIONS AND BEST PRACTICES*

Ladakh and the North East can benefit from adopting sustainable practices and innovative models tailored to their unique environmental and socio-economic contexts. Eco-friendly housing solutions, like Kerala's bamboo-reinforced construction, offer cost-effective and disaster-resilient alternatives. Integrated waste management systems, such as Indore's model emphasizing segregation at source, composting, and recycling, can significantly enhance urban sustainability in cities like Leh and Shillong. Participatory urban planning frameworks, inspired by Maharashtra's People's Plan Campaign, can foster inclusive decision-making. Green infrastructure initiatives, modeled after Bengaluru's Tree Parks, can improve air quality and public well-being in cities like Gangtok. Furthermore, scaling up solar energy adoption, based on Gujarat's Solar Rooftop Programme, can capitalize on the region's solar potential to promote renewable energy and reduce dependence on traditional sources.

## *Conclusion*

Ladakh and the North Eastern states exemplify the complexities of achieving SDG 11 due to their unique geographical and socio-economic contexts. While national policies and community efforts have initiated progress, challenges like unplanned urbanization, environmental degradation, and infrastructure deficits persist. By adopting innovative solutions and learning from successful models across India, these regions can create resilient, inclusive, and sustainable urban environments.

# SDG 12 – Responsible Consumption and Production: A Case Study on Goa and Delhi

Sustainable development relies heavily on the efficient use of resources and the minimization of environmental impacts, both of which form the core of SDG 12. Responsible consumption and production aim to ensure sustainable economic growth while maintaining ecological balance. In India, the challenges of achieving this goal are magnified by rapid urbanization, rising consumer demand, and economic inequalities. Goa and Delhi serve as distinct yet interconnected examples. Goa, with its reliance on tourism and mining, illustrates challenges in balancing economic benefits with environmental sustainability. Delhi, a densely populated urban center, faces issues such as waste management, pollution, and resource-intensive industrialization. Understanding these contexts offers insights into the complexities of achieving SDG 12 in diverse settings.

## Main Indicators of SDG 12

India's progress on SDG 12 is evaluated using indicators aligned with national and international frameworks. The following provide a snapshot of the relevant metrics:

1. **Material Footprint and Resource Efficiency**: India's material footprint per capita was estimated at 8.4 tons in 2020, lower than the global average of 12 tons but rising consistently (MoSPI, 2023). Resource efficiency, as measured by economic output per unit of resource input, is improving but remains below optimal levels in Goa and Delhi due to inefficiencies in industrial practices and urban resource management (UNEP,

2022).

2.  **Waste Generation and Management:** India generates over 62 million tons of municipal solid waste annually, of which only 20% is processed (CPCB, 2023). Goa produces approximately 0.3 million tons, while Delhi generates over 14,000 tons daily, reflecting stark differences in waste management needs.

3.  **Sustainable Tourism:** Tourism contributes significantly to Goa's GDP, accounting for 16.43% in 2022 (Goa Tourism Department, 2023). However, unregulated practices pose risks to natural ecosystems. Delhi's tourism is heritage-focused, creating opportunities for sustainable urban initiatives.

4.  **Policy Implementation and Awareness:** The enforcement of Extended Producer Responsibility (EPR) for e-waste and plastic waste management reflects a growing focus on accountability. Public awareness campaigns are critical but underfunded in both regions (NITI Aayog, 2023).

## *Current Policies and Initiatives*

### Resource Efficiency and Waste Management

The Sustainable Mining Initiative, in Goa, implemented in collaboration with the Indian Bureau of Mines, focuses on post-mining land rehabilitation and biodiversity restoration. However, monitoring mechanisms need strengthening to address illegal mining activities (Ministry of Mines, 2023). Goa's Integrated Solid Waste Management Project in Saligao processes mixed waste into compost and energy, showcasing effective technology adoption. The model is replicable but requires scaling up to manage seasonal surges in waste during peak tourist seasons (CPCB, 2023).

Delhi's Material Recovery Facilities (MRFs) segregate and recycle approximately 50% of municipal solid waste, significantly reducing landfill reliance (Delhi Urban Shelter Improvement Board, 2023). However, informal waste pickers, who handle a significant portion of recycling, lack formal recognition and social protections. Policies like the Graded Response Action Plan (GRAP) in Delhi address air pollution by restricting industrial activities and vehicular emissions during high smog periods. However, enforcement gaps remain.

**Pollution and Urbanization Challenges**

Goa's coastal ecosystems face degradation from unchecked tourism activities, with over 70% of its beaches experiencing moderate to severe erosion (National Centre for Sustainable Coastal Management, 2023). Pollution from cruise ships and water sports contributes to declining marine biodiversity. Efforts to reduce plastic waste include bans on single-use plastics and incentives for eco-friendly packaging. Despite these measures, illegal dumping persists in rural areas in Goa.

Delhi's industrial hubs contribute heavily to air and water pollution. Yamuna River rejuvenation projects, under schemes like Namami Gange, show limited success due to inadequate sewage treatment infrastructure (MoEFCC, 2023). The city's per capita carbon footprint is among the highest in India, exacerbated by high vehicular density and unplanned urban sprawl.

**Economic and Social Impacts**

Goa's tourism-dependent economy creates seasonal employment but lacks income stability, leading to higher economic vulnerability among rural communities. Delhi's high population density strains public services, exacerbating social inequalities. Informal settlements house 15% of its population, with limited access to clean water and sanitation (Census of India, 2021).

## *Challenges*

Goa's rural areas lack waste management infrastructure, while Delhi's peri-urban zones are neglected in urban planning frameworks. Goa's income inequality, though lower than Delhi's, results from a reliance on tourism-centric jobs. Delhi's informal labor sector suffers from precarious employment conditions. Weak monitoring mechanisms and insufficient funding hinder the effectiveness of waste management and pollution control policies in both regions.

**Recommendations and Best Practices from Other States and UTs**

Goa and Delhi can draw inspiration from various state initiatives to promote sustainable development and social equity. Kerala's Responsible Tourism Initiative, exemplified by the Kumarakom model, links local communities to the tourism supply chain, fostering economic empowerment and ecological sustainability—an approach adaptable to Goa's coastal tourism sector. Himachal Pradesh's Homestay Scheme integrates rural households into hospitality networks, offering eco-friendly tourism solutions that can benefit Delhi's peri-urban zones. Indore's decentralized waste management model, renowned for its efficiency in segregation, recycling, and composting, provides a replicable framework for improving waste management in both regions. Surat's green urban planning, emphasizing disaster resilience and sustainable infrastructure, serves as a blueprint for Delhi to manage urban sprawl. Strengthening monitoring and enforcement mechanisms for existing waste and pollution policies, promoting public-private partnerships for green infrastructure, formalizing informal sectors like waste pickers, and launching awareness campaigns on sustainable consumption are vital policy measures to support these adaptations.

**Conclusion**

SDG 12 underscores the need for systemic changes in consumption and production patterns. Goa and Delhi, despite their differing contexts, highlight the importance of integrating local initiatives with global sustainability goals. Adopting successful models from other states and focusing on community engagement, policy enforcement, and technological innovation can significantly advance India's progress toward responsible consumption and production.

# CHAPTER THIRTEEN

# SDG 13 – Climate Action: A Case Study of West Bengal, Andaman and Nicobar Islands, and Lakshadweep

Sustainable Development Goal 13 (SDG 13), "Climate Action," emphasizes the need to take urgent action to combat climate change and its impacts. In the context of India, addressing the challenges of climate change involves understanding regional vulnerabilities, implementing comprehensive climate policies, and promoting sustainable practices that align with global goals such as those set by the Paris Agreement. This chapter aims to explore the current state of climate action in West Bengal, Andaman & Nicobar Islands, and Lakshadweep, highlighting key indicators, challenges, policy interventions, and recommendations.

**Climate Vulnerabilities and Impacts**

India is particularly vulnerable to climate change due to its vast geographical spread and diverse ecosystems. The states and regions selected for this study—West Bengal, Andaman & Nicobar Islands, and Lakshadweep—are facing unique challenges due to their geographical locations and economic profiles.

### Disaster Preparedness

West Bengal, due to its vast coastline and proximity to the Bay of Bengal, is highly vulnerable to extreme weather events like cyclones, floods, and coastal erosion. The state has made significant strides in disaster preparedness, particularly in the wake of frequent cyclones like Amphan (2020) and Yaas (2021). The West Bengal Disaster Management Policy has been strengthened through the establishment of the West Bengal State Disaster Management Authority (WBSDMA), which coordinates disaster response and preparedness. The state's resilience strategy includes enhancing early warning systems, improving flood control infrastructure, and strengthening community-based disaster management systems. In terms of policy, the state has adhered to the guidelines set by the National Disaster Management Authority (NDMA) and implemented localized measures like the construction of embankments and the promotion of flood-resistant farming techniques. Moreover, the state's collaboration with the National Adaptation Fund for Climate Change (NAFCC) has funded several disaster mitigation projects, focusing on areas vulnerable to sea-level rise and cyclonic impacts.

The Andaman & Nicobar Islands, an archipelago in the Bay of Bengal, are highly prone to sea-level rise, storm surges, and tsunamis. The islands have developed the Andaman and Nicobar Islands Disaster Management Plan, which includes measures to strengthen coastal protection, improve infrastructure resilience, and enhance public awareness. The local government has installed tsunami warning systems and has worked on increasing community engagement for disaster preparedness. However, the region still faces challenges due to its remoteness, lack of sufficient infrastructure, and vulnerability to multiple natural hazards. Increased focus on integrated disaster risk management (IDRM) is necessary to ensure preparedness, response, and recovery in the face of climate change.

Lakshadweep, an archipelago of islands in the Arabian Sea, faces similar threats, including rising sea levels, salinity intrusion, and extreme weather events. The Disaster Management Plan for Lakshadweep emphasizes the vulnerability of its atolls and the need for heightened disaster response infrastructure. The islands are working on strengthening early warning systems, improving cyclone shelters, and introducing climate-resilient agriculture. Given its unique vulnerability, international collaboration and financial assistance, such as the Green Climate Fund, could aid in strengthening disaster preparedness.

**Renewable Energy**

West Bengal has taken steps towards integrating renewable energy into its power mix. The state has set targets for the installation of renewable energy capacity, focusing on solar, wind, and small hydro projects. By 2023, the state had achieved around 2.5 GW of renewable energy capacity, with a significant share coming from solar power. The government also promotes rooftop solar installations through subsidy schemes and incentives, helping to drive the shift towards cleaner energy. Despite these efforts, challenges remain in terms of grid integration and power distribution infrastructure, especially in rural areas. The state needs further investments in renewable energy infrastructure and smart grid technology to meet the growing demand for green energy.

The Andaman & Nicobar Islands are heavily dependent on fossil fuels for electricity, but there has been a push towards renewable energy, particularly solar. The islands have set ambitious targets to harness solar power, with the installation of over 2 MW of solar capacity by 2023. The government has also focused on making the islands energy self-sufficient by exploring the potential of tidal and wave energy, given the abundance of water bodies surrounding the islands. However, the islands face logistical challenges in scaling up renewable energy due to their geographical location and limited infrastructure. Investments in decentralized energy systems and microgrids can help address these challenges.

Lakshadweep, with its small and dispersed population, has a great potential for renewable energy, particularly solar power. The government of Lakshadweep has implemented the "Green Energy Initiative," aiming to reduce the islands' reliance on diesel for electricity generation. The initiative focuses on deploying solar power plants and battery storage systems across the islands, with a target to achieve 100% renewable energy by 2030. However, achieving this ambitious target requires addressing challenges related to storage, transmission, and high operational costs.

**Pollution Control and Industry Compliance**

West Bengal's industrialization has significantly contributed to air and water pollution, particularly in Kolkata and other urban centers. The state has taken steps to mitigate pollution through various initiatives under the State Action Plan on Climate Change (SAPCC) and the Clean Air Action Plan. West Bengal is also working towards reducing vehicular emissions by promoting electric vehicles (EVs) and improving public transportation systems. In terms of industrial compliance, the West Bengal Pollution Control Board (WBPCB) enforces environmental regulations concerning air quality, water management, and waste disposal. Despite these efforts, there are challenges related to the effective implementation of environmental standards and monitoring industrial pollution.

Both the Andaman & Nicobar Islands and Lakshadweep face less industrial pollution compared to mainland India. However, with rising tourism and commercial activity, these regions are witnessing an increase in waste generation, water pollution, and pressure on natural resources. Policies and frameworks to ensure waste management, water conservation, and the preservation of coral reefs are being strengthened. These territories need to implement more robust mechanisms for waste management and pollution control to mitigate the risks posed by increasing tourism and climate change.

### Climate Action Indicators and Progress

### Greenhouse Gas Emissions and Carbon Footprint

India's carbon emissions have seen a steady increase, which aligns with the country's growing industrial base and energy needs. In the case of West Bengal, emissions have been largely driven by industrialization, urbanization, and the energy sector. The state has witnessed a significant rise in transportation emissions and electricity consumption.

The islands of Andaman & Nicobar and Lakshadweep, though less industrialized, face the brunt of climate impacts through increased vulnerability rather than significant emissions. Their carbon footprint is relatively low, but the risk of environmental degradation due to climate change necessitates action in sustainable resource management and energy consumption.

### National Adaptation Plans and National Missions

India's National Action Plan on Climate Change (NAPCC), which lays the framework for climate action across the country, focuses on eight key missions, including the National Mission on Sustainable Agriculture, National Mission on Sustainable Habitat, and the National Mission on Water. In West Bengal, the implementation of these missions is critical for adapting to climate change. The state has made progress through programs that enhance water conservation, promote energy efficiency, and encourage sustainable agriculture practices.

The Andaman & Nicobar Islands and Lakshadweep have also adopted some aspects of these missions, focusing on preserving biodiversity, enhancing water security, and promoting renewable energy initiatives, such as solar power, to reduce dependence on fossil fuels.

**Nationally Determined Contributions (NDCs) and Net Zero Emissions**

India's Nationally Determined Contributions (NDCs), as part of the Paris Agreement, set a clear roadmap for reducing carbon emissions, increasing the share of renewable energy, and achieving net-zero emissions by 2070. In line with India's national commitments, the states and union territories like West Bengal and Lakshadweep are focusing on transitioning to green energy, promoting renewable energy adoption, and improving energy efficiency. These goals are mirrored in local efforts to meet NDC targets.

## Challenges

### Social and Economic Impacts

The challenges of climate change disproportionately affect marginalized communities, especially in coastal and island regions. In West Bengal, the impacts of cyclones and flooding have led to displacement and loss of livelihoods, particularly in rural areas. Similarly, in the islands of Andaman & Nicobar and Lakshadweep, the loss of biodiversity and resources threatens local economies reliant on tourism and fisheries.

Additionally, the economic impacts of climate change in the form of reduced agricultural productivity, especially in rural areas, create pressures on livelihoods, public health, and food security. The cost of adapting to climate change remains a critical concern, particularly for vulnerable populations.

**Resource Consumption and Waste Management**

Increased industrial activity and urbanization in West Bengal have exacerbated issues of resource consumption, waste generation, and improper waste management. As the state continues to grow, managing waste and reducing resource consumption remain major challenges. Similarly, in island territories, waste management infrastructure is limited, and there is an over-reliance on fossil fuels for energy generation, contributing to environmental degradation.

**Carbon Credit and Green Energy Transition**

India's efforts to integrate carbon credit systems and the promotion of green energy are crucial for the success of SDG 13. West Bengal, with its industrial sector, faces the challenge of balancing economic growth with emissions reductions. Efforts to expand renewable energy sources, including solar power and wind energy, are vital to reducing the carbon footprint. In the islands, the promotion of solar energy has gained traction due to the availability of abundant sunlight and the need for energy independence. However, challenges remain in terms of energy storage and grid connectivity.

## *Policy Frameworks and Initiatives*

1. **National Adaptation Fund for Climate Change (NAFCC):** The NAFCC provides funding for climate change adaptation projects. West Bengal has used this fund for various disaster management initiatives, including flood control, water management, and soil conservation. Similarly, in Andaman & Nicobar and Lakshadweep, NAFCC has been used to promote resilience-building activities, such as coastal erosion prevention and sustainable fisheries.

2. **Climate Change Action Programme (CCAP):** The CCAP focuses on integrated climate action and fostering resilience. West Bengal has incorporated CCAP initiatives in urban planning and infrastructure development. In the island regions, CCAP-related activities focus on enhancing local adaptation capacity through sustainable agriculture practices and disaster management planning.

3. **Green Climate Fund (GCF) and National Clean Energy Fund (NCEF):** The Green Climate Fund supports projects that mitigate and adapt to climate change. West Bengal has utilized this fund for large-scale renewable energy projects and urban resilience initiatives. The NCEF supports the transition to clean energy, and the state's focus on solar and wind energy aligns with national climate action goals.

4. **Atal Mission for Rejuvenation and Urban Transformation (AMRUT):** AMRUT, launched in 2015, focuses on providing basic infrastructure services in urban areas, including water supply, sanitation, drainage systems, and green spaces. By improving urban

infrastructure, AMRUT also enhances cities' resilience to climate change impacts. West Bengal has leveraged AMRUT to improve urban amenities, particularly in Kolkata, through projects such as the installation of energy-efficient LED street lights, promotion of green spaces, and the construction of sewage treatment plants (Ministry of Housing and Urban Affairs, 2020). These efforts align with SDG 13 by improving climate resilience and reducing urban carbon footprints.The state has also initiated several climate-conscious urban mobility projects, such as electric buses and cycle-sharing systems, which contribute to reducing emissions and enhancing sustainable urban transport networks (West Bengal State Action Plan on Climate Change, 2020).

5. **Faster Adoption and Manufacturing of Hybrid and Electric Vehicles (FAME):** The FAME scheme, introduced by the Ministry of Heavy Industries and Public Enterprises, aims to boost the adoption of electric vehicles (EVs) through financial incentives and infrastructure development. This policy contributes to reducing vehicular emissions, a significant source of air pollution and carbon emissions in urban centers. West Bengal has actively engaged with the FAME initiative by setting up EV charging infrastructure and incentivizing electric bus fleets for public transport in Kolkata (Ministry of Heavy Industries and Public Enterprises, 2021).Electric vehicles, particularly in Kolkata, have grown in popularity, with a noticeable increase in electric rickshaws and buses, helping improve air quality and reduce the region's carbon footprint (NITI Aayog, 2021).

6. **National Renewable Energy Mission (NREMs):** The National Renewable Energy Mission, launched in 2010, aims to accelerate renewable energy development in India, with a goal of achieving 500 GW of renewable energy capacity by 2030 (Ministry of New and Renewable Energy, 2021). West Bengal, rich in renewable resources, particularly solar and wind, has made significant strides toward meeting this target, installing approximately 2.5 GW of renewable energy capacity by 2023 (West Bengal Renewable Energy Development Agency, 2023).The state's government has introduced policies to support solar installations in both rural and urban areas, including tax incentives and subsidies for rooftop solar installations and the promotion of decentralized solar power generation (NITI Aayog, 2021). These initiatives are in line with India's overarching goal to transition to a low-carbon energy future.

7. **National Solar Mission (NSM):** India's National Solar Mission, a part of its broader renewable energy strategy, aims to achieve 100 GW of solar power capacity by 2022 (Ministry of New and Renewable Energy, 2021). West Bengal has made significant progress in solar energy generation, supported by the NSM framework, with the state focusing on large-scale solar parks and rooftop solar systems in urban and rural areas (West Bengal Solar Policy, 2022). The Andaman & Nicobar Islands and Lakshadweep, both of which face energy access challenges, are also making strides toward enhancing solar energy capacity, particularly through decentralized energy systems that provide reliable power to remote areas.Lakshadweep, in particular, is aiming for a 100% renewable energy target by 2030,

with solar power playing a critical role in its energy transition (Lakshadweep Renewable Energy Development Agency, 2021).

**State and UT Policies**

**1. West Bengal's State Action Plan on Climate Change (SAPCC)**

West Bengal's SAPCC outlines strategies to address climate change across various sectors such as water, agriculture, forestry, and energy. The SAPCC is closely aligned with the NAPCC (National Action Plan on Climate Change) and supports SDG 13 by prioritizing climate-resilient agriculture, water conservation, and energy efficiency (West Bengal State Action Plan on Climate Change, 2020). Among its key initiatives are the promotion of solar energy, rainwater harvesting, and the conservation of natural resources like wetlands and forests.

The state has also adopted climate-resilient urban infrastructure measures, including green spaces and sustainable waste management practices in major cities such as Kolkata (West Bengal State Action Plan on Climate Change, 2020).

**2. Climate Adaptation Strategy of Andaman & Nicobar Islands**

Given its vulnerability to climate change, particularly sea-level rise and cyclonic storms, the Andaman & Nicobar Islands have developed a comprehensive climate change adaptation strategy. This includes a disaster management plan focused on ecosystem restoration and the construction of resilient infrastructure. The region is working on the rehabilitation of mangroves and coral reefs, both of which play a critical role in coastal protection (Andaman and Nicobar Islands Administration, 2021).

Additionally, the government has supported the adoption of solar energy systems across the islands to reduce dependency on diesel generators, with many remote islands now integrating solar-based microgrids to ensure energy access while reducing emissions (Andaman and Nicobar Islands Administration, 2021).

**3. Lakshadweep's Green Energy Initiative**

Lakshadweep's Green Energy Initiative is one of India's most ambitious renewable energy programs, targeting 100% renewable energy by 2030. This initiative promotes solar power and battery storage solutions, significantly reducing the need for imported fossil fuels (Lakshadweep Renewable Energy Development Agency, 2021). The islands are also implementing energy-efficient practices, such as the use of LED lighting and promoting low-carbon transport options.

The Green Energy Initiative has been particularly successful in integrating solar power with local community needs, reducing energy costs, and creating sustainable livelihoods through the provision of renewable energy (Lakshadweep Renewable Energy Development Agency, 2021).

## *Community Initiatives*

### 1. Community-Based Disaster Risk Management (CBDRM) in West Bengal

West Bengal has prioritized community-based disaster risk management (CBDRM) to enhance local preparedness for climate-related hazards such as floods, cyclones, and droughts. Local communities are engaged in disaster preparedness activities, including early warning systems, evacuation protocols, and post-disaster recovery planning

(West Bengal State Disaster Management Authority, 2020).

These community-driven initiatives ensure that local populations are better equipped to manage the risks posed by climate change and contribute to the state's overall climate resilience.

**2. Coastal Protection and Community Engagement in Andaman & Nicobar Islands**

Community engagement is central to the Andaman & Nicobar Islands' approach to climate adaptation. Local populations are involved in efforts to protect coastal ecosystems, particularly through mangrove restoration and coral reef conservation (Andaman and Nicobar Islands Administration, 2021). These initiatives are not only environmentally beneficial but also provide alternative livelihoods through eco-tourism and sustainable resource management.

**3. Community-Driven Renewable Energy Projects in Lakshadweep**

Lakshadweep's community-driven renewable energy projects focus on solar power installations managed and maintained by local communities. This decentralized approach has significantly improved energy access while empowering islanders to take ownership of their energy systems (Lakshadweep Renewable Energy Development Agency, 2021). These efforts support the broader objective of achieving 100% renewable energy by 2030, contributing to the region's sustainable development goals.

## *Recommendations and Best Practices*

To ensure better disaster preparedness, it is essential to enhance early warning systems, invest in climate-resilient infrastructure, and promote community-based disaster management, particularly in West Bengal, Andaman & Nicobar, and Lakshadweep. These measures will help mitigate the impacts of future climate events and ensure communities are better equipped to handle natural disasters. In parallel, expanding renewable energy sources like solar, wind, and hydroelectric power, especially in island regions, will reduce reliance on fossil fuels, align with India's Nationally Determined Contributions (NDCs), and support long-term sustainability. Additionally, implementing decentralized energy systems and storage solutions is crucial to address the specific needs of remote areas.

Another key focus should be strengthening pollution control measures by ensuring stricter industrial compliance with environmental standards. Promoting green technologies and improving waste management systems are vital steps in reducing pollution in urban and industrial zones. Adopting a more sustainable approach to waste and resource management will contribute significantly to improving environmental quality across these regions.

The success stories from various states offer valuable insights for replication. Sikkim, for instance, has made significant strides in sustainable agriculture, forest conservation, and hydroelectric power development, providing a solid model for agricultural states like West Bengal. Meghalaya's community-based conservation efforts and renewable energy promotion, particularly hydropower, offer useful strategies for island territories like Andaman & Nicobar. Similarly, Tamil Nadu's leadership in renewable energy, especially wind and solar, coupled with its focus on energy efficiency and industrial sustainability, presents key lessons for West Bengal.

Kerala's integrated waste management system, renewable energy initiatives, and community-driven environmental protection strategies are particularly relevant for island regions such as Andaman & Nicobar and Lakshadweep. Additionally, Karnataka's success in integrated watershed management and agroforestry, which boosts agricultural productivity while minimizing environmental impact, can serve as a model for West Bengal and the island territories. By adopting community-based natural resource management and strengthening climate resilience, these regions can effectively promote sustainable development.

## *Conclusion*

SDG 13 – Climate Action, presents an urgent call for global and local efforts to mitigate and adapt to climate change. West Bengal, Andaman & Nicobar Islands, and Lakshadweep are at the frontline of this challenge, with their unique vulnerabilities and opportunities. By leveraging national policies, international funds, and local initiatives, these regions can enhance their resilience to climate change while contributing to global climate goals. The integration of sustainable practices and active community engagement will be key to achieving long-term climate resilience and fostering sustainable development.

# CHAPTER FOURTEEN

# SDG 14 – Life Below Water: A Case Study on Gujarat

Sustainable Development Goal (SDG) 14, Life Below Water, aims to conserve and sustainably use the oceans, seas, and marine resources for sustainable development.

India, with its vast coastline of 7,517 kilometers, is home to significant marine biodiversity and relies heavily on its marine and coastal ecosystems for livelihood, food security, and economic growth. Gujarat, one of India's key coastal states, plays a crucial role in meeting SDG 14 targets. This chapter explores Gujarat's progress in achieving SDG 14 through an analysis of marine biodiversity, water quality, pollution control, aquaculture, and mangrove conservation. It examines national and state policies, community initiatives, and best practices from other regions that could enhance Gujarat's efforts toward sustaining life below water.

## *Gujarat's Marine Ecosystem and Biodiversity*

### 1. Marine Biodiversity and Coastal Ecosystems

Gujarat's coastline is one of the most ecologically rich in India, supporting a variety of marine species, including fish, crustaceans, and mollusks. The state is also home to the Gulf of Kutch and the Gulf of Khambhat, both of which are rich in marine life. However, the state's marine biodiversity is under threat from pollution, overfishing, and habitat degradation.

The marine ecosystems in Gujarat include coral reefs, mangrove forests, seagrasses, and estuaries. These ecosystems are critical for supporting marine life, providing breeding grounds for fish, and offering coastal protection from storms and erosion. The National Biodiversity Action Plan (NBAP) emphasizes the importance of conserving marine biodiversity, which has been implemented through various marine protected areas (MPAs) in Gujarat, including the Gulf of Kutch Marine National Park (Ministry of Environment, Forest and

Climate Change [MoEFCC], 2018).

## 2. Mangrove Conservation

Mangroves are essential for both coastal protection and the sustainable management of marine resources. Gujarat has one of the largest areas of mangrove forests in India, particularly along its Saurashtra coast and in the Gulf of Kutch. These forests act as carbon sinks, protect coastlines from erosion, and support marine biodiversity.

Recent studies have shown that Gujarat's mangrove coverage has increased due to focused conservation efforts. The Gujarat Forest Department, in collaboration with national agencies like the MoEFCC, has initiated several projects to conserve and expand mangrove ecosystems, such as the **Mangrove Afforestation and Conservation Project (MPEDA, 2021)**. Under the **National Afforestation Programme**, Gujarat has seen an increase in its mangrove coverage, contributing to the mitigation of coastal erosion and providing habitats for numerous marine species (Ministry of Environment, Forest and Climate Change [MoEFCC], 2021).

Moreover, Gujarat's **Mangrove and Coastal Biodiversity Conservation Project**, launched with the support of the World Bank, has been aimed at restoring degraded mangrove areas and enhancing coastal biodiversity management (World Bank, 2020).

Despite challenges such as land reclamation and industrial development, these efforts have helped restore significant areas of mangrove forests in the state.

# *Water Quality and Pollution Management*

## 1. Water Quality in Coastal Areas

Water quality in Gujarat's coastal regions is critical for both the health of marine ecosystems and the livelihood of coastal communities dependent on fishing. High Biological Oxygen Demand (BOD) levels and the presence of harmful chemicals from industrial discharges have raised concerns regarding coastal water quality. According to the Central Pollution Control Board (CPCB), several locations along Gujarat's coastline, such as those near Surat and Bhavnagar, face issues of high pollution levels, primarily from untreated industrial effluents and agricultural runoff (CPCB, 2020).

The Gujarat Pollution Control Board (GPCB) monitors coastal water quality and has implemented measures to reduce industrial effluents. The state has also collaborated with the national Clean Ganga Mission and the Swachh Bharat Kosh for improving sanitation and pollution control, which indirectly benefits the coastal and marine ecosystems (MoEFCC, 2020).

## 2. Industrial Effluents and Fertilizer Runoff

Industrial growth in Gujarat, particularly in sectors such as textiles, chemicals, and petrochemicals, has led to significant pollution in coastal areas. The discharge of untreated industrial effluents into rivers and coastal waters poses a serious threat to marine life. Similarly, fertilizers and pesticides from agriculture run off into the sea, leading to nutrient overload and eutrophication.

The Gujarat Government has implemented several pollution control measures, including the establishment of effluent treatment plants and stricter enforcement of environmental norms for industries. The National Plan for the Conservation of Aquatic Ecosystems (NPCA) is being applied to reduce pollution levels in critical aquatic ecosystems along the coastline (Ministry of Water Resources, 2021).

## *Aquaculture and Fisheries*

### 1. Aquaculture in Gujarat

Aquaculture is a vital sector in Gujarat, contributing to both the state's economy and food security. Gujarat is a major producer of shrimp, fish, and other marine species. The state has developed a robust aquaculture industry, particularly in the Saurashtra region, where shrimp farming is a key economic activity. However, the expansion of aquaculture poses risks to marine ecosystems, such as mangrove destruction, water pollution, and the spread of disease among marine species.

The Gujarat government has initiated sustainable aquaculture practices, including the promotion of **integrated coastal zone management (ICZM)** and the development of eco-friendly aquaculture models. These initiatives align with the National Fisheries Policy, which emphasizes sustainable practices in the aquaculture sector (Ministry of Fisheries, Animal Husbandry and Dairying, 2020).

**Gujarat Coastal Zone Management Plan (GCZMP)**

Gujarat's Coastal Zone Management Plan (GCZMP) is an essential tool for balancing industrial development with environmental conservation along its coastline. The plan focuses on regulating coastal activities to reduce environmental degradation, particularly from unregulated construction, mining, and industrial activities. The GCZMP ensures that development activities along the coast comply with environmental regulations set out in the Environment Protection Act (EPA), 1986, and the Coastal Regulation

Zone (CRZ) Notification, 2011.

The GCZMP also supports efforts to manage waste and pollutants that may be discharged into coastal waters, thus helping to improve water quality and protect marine ecosystems from chemical and plastic pollution (Gujarat Pollution Control Board [GPCB], 2020). Additionally, the Gujarat Maritime Board (GMB) oversees the establishment and enforcement of environmental standards for port development, ensuring that sustainable practices are adopted in coastal industrial areas (GMB, 2020).

**2. Fishing Practices and Overfishing**

Fishing is a major livelihood activity for many coastal communities in Gujarat. However, overfishing, especially the exploitation of non-renewable marine resources, has led to the depletion of fish stocks and disruption of marine food chains. The state's fisheries department has implemented several measures to address overfishing, such as fishing bans during breeding seasons and the promotion of sustainable fishing gear.

The Gujarat State Fisheries policy includes guidelines for the responsible management of fish stocks, the use of sustainable fishing practices, and the protection of critical habitats such as mangroves and coral reefs. It also outlines the development of aquaculture practices that are environmentally sustainable and economically viable (Gujarat Fisheries Department, 2020).

The Gujarat Fisheries Development Corporation (GFDC) has also been instrumental in implementing the state's fisheries policies. The GFDC supports the growth of both marine and freshwater aquaculture, focusing on improving production techniques and market linkages, while also ensuring the protection of aquatic ecosystems (GFDC, 2021).

Gujarat is also focusing on strengthening its Marine Protected Areas (MPAs) and the establishment of no-catch zones, which will help restore fish populations and ensure sustainable fisheries. Pradhan Mantri Matsya Sampada Yojana (PMMSY) by the Department of Fisheries under Ministry of Fisheries, Animal Husbandry, and Dairying is aimed at enhancing sustainable fisheries and promoting responsible fishing (Ministry of Fisheries, Animal Husbandry and Dairying, 2021).

## *National Policies*

### Sagarmala Project

The Sagarmala Project is a national initiative aimed at enhancing port connectivity, reducing logistics costs, and promoting industrial growth along India's coastline. While the project focuses on infrastructure development, it also addresses environmental concerns related to coastal development, such as the impact of ports and shipping activities on marine ecosystems. In Gujarat, several initiatives under Sagarmala focus on enhancing the environmental sustainability of ports through the introduction of green technologies and sustainable port practices (Ministry of Shipping, 2020).

### National Plan for the Conservation of Aquatic Ecosystems

The National Plan for the Conservation of Aquatic Ecosystems (NPCA) provides a framework for conserving India's aquatic ecosystems, including Gujarat's coastal and marine areas. This plan emphasizes water quality management, habitat restoration, and sustainable management of aquatic resources. Gujarat has implemented several projects under the NPCA, focusing on reducing pollution from industrial and agricultural activities and enhancing the ecological health of coastal ecosystems (MoEFCC, 2020).

## Community Initiatives

Community-based marine conservation initiatives in Gujarat, such as those led by local NGOs and fisherfolk organizations, have proven to be effective in enhancing marine resource management. These initiatives focus on community awareness, sustainable fishing practices, and the protection of coastal ecosystems like mangroves and coral reefs. The active participation of local communities in marine conservation has contributed to the state's progress toward achieving SDG 14 (CSE, 2021).

## Best Practices from Other States

States like West Bengal have implemented successful models for integrating community-based fisheries management and habitat conservation, which Gujarat could replicate. For example, the state has focused on sustainable aquaculture practices and community engagement in marine conservation, which has led to healthier marine ecosystems and better fish stocks (West Bengal Fisheries Department, 2020). Similarly, Kerala's initiatives to protect mangroves and coastal ecosystems, alongside its strong focus on water quality management, offer valuable insights for Gujarat to enhance its marine resource conservation efforts.

## Conclusion

Gujarat plays a pivotal role in achieving SDG 14 due to its vast coastline, rich marine biodiversity, and significant dependence on fisheries and aquaculture. The state has made considerable progress in conserving marine ecosystems, improving water quality, and adopting sustainable aquaculture practices. However, challenges such as industrial pollution, overfishing, and the degradation of coastal habitats remain. By continuing to strengthen marine protected areas, enhancing pollution control measures, and engaging local communities in conservation efforts, Gujarat can contribute significantly to India's commitment to SDG 14.

Gujarat's policies and initiatives, in alignment with national efforts such as the Sagarmala Project, the NPCA, and the Pradhan Mantri Matsya Sampada Yojana, will help ensure sustainable use of marine resources and the protection of life below water. Best practices from other states, such as West Bengal, will further bolster Gujarat's ongoing efforts toward achieving a sustainable future for its coastal and marine ecosystems.

# CHAPTER FIFTEEN

# SDG 15 – Life on Land: A Case Study on Ladakh and Jammu & Kashmir

Sustainable Development Goal (SDG) 15, Life on Land, seeks to combat desertification, halt and reverse land degradation, and halt biodiversity loss. In India, Ladakh and Jammu & Kashmir represent unique ecosystems that contribute significantly to biodiversity conservation and natural resource management. These regions face challenges such as land degradation, loss of biodiversity, and desertification due to climate change, human activity, and unsustainable development practices. This chapter explores the status of SDG 15 in Ladakh and Jammu & Kashmir, examining national and state policies, initiatives, and the challenges faced by these regions in terms of land management, biodiversity protection, and afforestation efforts.

## *Key Indicators*

### 1. Forest Cover and Carbon Stock

In Ladakh and Jammu & Kashmir, the landscape is largely characterized by high-altitude mountains, wetlands, and arid terrain, with limited forest cover. The Forest Survey of India (FSI), in its latest report, indicates that Jammu & Kashmir has a total forest cover of 20.62% of its geographical area, which includes both temperate forests in the foothills and alpine forests in the higher reaches. However, the proportion of forest cover in Ladakh is minimal, with arid zones and desert landscapes dominating the region (FSI, 2019).

While tree cover in Jammu & Kashmir is stable, there are concerns regarding the degradation of forests due to illegal logging, livestock grazing, and encroachment (Ministry of Environment, Forest and Climate Change [MoEFCC], 2020). In Ladakh, the importance of carbon sequestration through vegetation is recognized, especially as the region faces increasing temperatures and shifting weather patterns.

## 2. Degradation of Land and Desertification

Land degradation is a significant challenge in both Jammu & Kashmir and Ladakh, where agricultural practices and urban expansion contribute to desertification and soil erosion. According to the Desertification and Land Degradation Atlas of India, Ladakh is classified as one of the most vulnerable areas in terms of desertification. The region's fragile ecosystem is sensitive to climate change, and the increasing human settlements and infrastructure development contribute to soil erosion and degradation of arable land (MoEFCC, 2016). Similarly, in Jammu & Kashmir, the Rural Development and Panchayati Raj Department notes that over-extraction of water resources for irrigation and mining activities has exacerbated land degradation in certain areas (Rural Development Ministry, 2020).

## 3. Biodiversity and Wildlife Conservation

Jammu & Kashmir and Ladakh are home to a rich variety of flora and fauna, including species such as the Himalayan brown bear, snow leopard, and kiang (wild ass). The region's wetlands, such as Hokersar and Wullar Lake, are important habitats for migratory birds, particularly during the winter months. However, wildlife crimes, such as poaching and illegal trade of endangered species, remain a challenge despite efforts to improve protection. The National Tiger Conservation Authority (NTCA) and the Wildlife Protection Act (1972) provide frameworks for wildlife protection, but enforcement is often weak due to the difficult terrain and lack of infrastructure (NTCA, 2020).

Ladakh, in particular, faces threats from invasive species, which impact native flora and fauna. The introduction of non-native plant species, along with climate shifts, has disrupted local ecosystems and biodiversity. Both regions are also experiencing the effects of climate change, leading to altered migration patterns of wildlife and shifts in biodiversity (World Bank, 2020).

## *National Policies*

### 1. National Forest Policy, 1988

The National Forest Policy (1988) focuses on increasing the area under forest cover, improving forest quality, and addressing issues like land degradation and biodiversity loss. Jammu & Kashmir has aligned its state forest policies with the central guidelines, working towards afforestation and the protection of forests. However, the implementation of these policies faces challenges in Ladakh due to its arid climate and limited vegetation (MoEFCC, 2018). Community participation in forest management has been vital in the state, with initiatives like Joint Forest Management Committees (JFMCs) being successful in certain areas.

### 2. National Environmental Policy, 2006

The National Environmental Policy (2006) emphasizes the sustainable management of land resources and the protection of biodiversity. The policy's focus on integrated land-use planning and the prevention of desertification is pertinent for both Ladakh and Jammu & Kashmir, where land management practices are critical. While Jammu & Kashmir has made strides in implementing the policy, Ladakh faces challenges due to its rugged terrain and remoteness. The policy advocates for community-based natural resource management, which has been adopted in certain parts of Jammu & Kashmir for forest and water management (MoEFCC, 2006).

### 3. Green India Mission (GIM)

The Green India Mission, one of the eight national missions under the National Action Plan on Climate Change (NAPCC), seeks to increase forest cover and enhance carbon sequestration. Jammu & Kashmir has actively participated in the GIM by focusing on reforestation and afforestation activities. Ladakh, with its limited forest cover, has focused on afforestation and restoration of degraded landscapes, particularly in the Leh and Kargil districts (MoEFCC, 2020). The involvement of local communities in afforestation projects has been crucial for the success of these initiatives.

### 4. Project Elephant and Integrated Development of Wildlife Habitats

The Project Elephant, a national initiative, aims to conserve elephant habitats, mitigate human-elephant conflict, and improve the management of elephant corridors. Jammu & Kashmir, although not home to a significant elephant population, has integrated similar wildlife conservation strategies under the Integrated Development of Wildlife Habitats scheme. Ladakh's focus is primarily on conserving endangered species like the snow leopard, with projects funded under the National Wildlife Action Plan and Project Snow Leopard (NTCA, 2019).

### 5. National Afforestation Programme (NAP)

The National Afforestation Programme promotes afforestation and reforestation in degraded forest areas. Jammu & Kashmir has been actively involved in NAP to restore degraded forest landscapes, focusing on soil erosion control and the rehabilitation of barren land. In Ladakh, afforestation is challenging due to the cold desert climate, but innovative methods, such as using drought-resistant species, have been adopted to restore degraded areas (MoEFCC, 2020).

## *BEST PRACTICES FROM OTHER STATES/ UTs*

The Union Territory of Dadra and Nagar Haveli and Daman and Diu has adopted community-driven approaches to afforestation. The Joint Forest Management (JFM) model has been implemented with the active participation of local communities. The UT has been successful in increasing the green cover in areas that were previously degraded due to overgrazing and deforestation (Ministry of Environment, Forest and Climate Change [MoEFCC], 2019). Jharkhand has also focused on wildlife conservation by expanding its network of wildlife sanctuaries and national parks, including Betla National Park and Hazaribagh Wildlife Sanctuary. The state has developed effective strategies to mitigate human-wildlife conflicts, especially in areas inhabited by tigers and elephants (Wildlife Institute of India [WII], 2020).

The state of Tripura has focused on conserving its rich biodiversity by establishing several wildlife sanctuaries and promoting eco-tourism. For example, the Sepahijala Wildlife Sanctuary and Trishna Wildlife Sanctuary have become key areas for the conservation of rare species like the clouded leopard and Hoolock gibbons (Tripura Forest Department, 2019).

Tripura has successfully implemented integrated watershed management projects that focus on reforestation and soil conservation. These projects have played a significant role in combating land degradation and improving the health of water resources (MoEFCC, 2018).

Tripura has integrated agroforestry into its agricultural practices to prevent soil erosion and enhance biodiversity. By planting trees alongside crops, the state has reduced the impact of deforestation and soil degradation (Tripura Forest Department, 2020). This practice also helps increase carbon sequestration and promotes soil health.

Jharkhand has effectively implemented the Forest Rights Act (FRA), which provides local communities with legal rights over forest resources. This has enabled communities to manage forests sustainably while benefiting from their resources. The CFR has been instrumental in reducing illegal logging and promoting sustainable forest management practices (MoEFCC, 2020).

While not directly applicable to Ladakh and Jammu & Kashmir, initiatives like Harit Haryana Yojana can serve as a model for afforestation in the region. Under this scheme, Haryana has seen significant success in community-driven tree plantation activities. A similar approach could be adopted in Ladakh and Jammu & Kashmir, where local communities actively participate in the restoration of degraded lands and forests (Haryana Government, 2020).

The Shambhar Koti Lagwad Yojana in Maharashtra is another best practice that could be applied in Jammu & Kashmir and Ladakh. This program promotes large-scale tree plantation in urban and rural areas, and the involvement of community groups has been key to its success. The program's emphasis on local involvement could be replicated in Ladakh, where community-driven approaches to afforestation could help mitigate the effects of land degradation (Maharashtra Government, 2020).

## *Conclusion*

Ladakh and Jammu & Kashmir, with their unique landscapes and biodiversity, face significant challenges in achieving SDG 15. These regions are grappling with issues such as land degradation, desertification, deforestation, and wildlife conservation. However, national and state-level policies, such as the National Forest Policy, National Environmental Policy, and the Green India Mission, have played an important role in addressing these challenges. Local community initiatives have also contributed to land and biodiversity conservation.

To further progress toward SDG 15, both regions must focus on the implementation of integrated land management strategies, promote afforestation using climate-resilient species, and strengthen wildlife protection efforts. Collaboration with national programs and the adoption of best practices from other states will be crucial in overcoming the challenges faced by Ladakh and Jammu & Kashmir in the path toward sustainable land management and biodiversity conservation.

# CHAPTER SIXTEEN

# SDG 16 - Peace, Justice and Strong Institutions: A Case Study on Delhi, Jharkhand, and Odisha

Sustainable Development Goal (SDG) 16, which focuses on "Peace, Justice, and Strong Institutions," aims to promote peaceful societies, ensure access to justice for all, and build accountable and inclusive institutions. Achieving this goal is fundamental to securing the other SDGs, as peace and effective institutions are key to addressing issues like poverty, inequality, and environmental degradation. This chapter focuses on a detailed analysis of SDG 16 in the states of Delhi, Jharkhand, and Odisha, which have made significant strides in improving governance, human rights, and social justice, but still face challenges in these areas. The chapter discusses key indicators, policies, community initiatives, and best practices from these states to provide a comprehensive understanding of the progress and challenges under SDG 16.

**Main Indicators**

SDG 16 encompasses several key indicators that contribute to building peaceful societies and strong institutions. These indicators include:

1. Violence Reduction: Efforts to reduce violence, including domestic violence, hate crimes, and communal violence.
2. Human Rights: Ensuring the protection and promotion of human rights, particularly for vulnerable groups like refugees, Scheduled Tribes (STs), and marginalized communities.
3. Access to Justice: Strengthening judicial systems to provide access to fair and timely justice for all.
4. Corruption Control: Addressing corruption at all levels of government to ensure transparency and accountability in institutions.

5.  Social Justice and Equality: Promoting social justice through policies that address discrimination and inequality, particularly for marginalized and oppressed groups.
6.  Information Access: Ensuring free and open access to information and fostering media freedom.

## Case Study 1: Delhi

Delhi, as the national capital, plays a critical role in shaping policies related to peace, justice, and institutions. The city has a diverse population and significant challenges related to governance, human rights, and social justice.

**Key Aspects and Challenges**

1.  Violence and Human Rights: Delhi has faced significant challenges related to communal violence, gender-based violence, and rights violations. The Delhi riots in 2020 highlighted the fragility of peace in a multi-ethnic society. Despite being a hub for international diplomacy and human rights discourse, there remain widespread issues of discrimination, particularly affecting minorities and economically marginalized communities (National Human Rights Commission [NHRC], 2020).
2.  Access to Justice: Delhi has been making efforts to streamline its judicial system, but delays and backlog of cases remain major issues. The Delhi Legal Services Authority (DLSA) has been instrumental in providing free legal aid to the underprivileged, although challenges remain in terms of capacity and public awareness (Delhi Judicial Academy, 2019).

3. Corruption: While Delhi has implemented various measures to curb corruption, challenges persist, particularly in urban administration and police services. The Delhi Anti-Corruption Bureau (ACB) has taken steps to improve accountability, but the need for further reforms is evident in the way corruption cases are handled and the lack of independency and transparency of administrative processes (CVC Report, 2021).

**Policies and Initiatives**

1. Delhi Police Reform: Delhi has undertaken reforms to improve police accountability and responsiveness. The Delhi Police Act and the Police Reforms Committee have been key in this regard, though further implementation and reforms are needed (Ministry of Home Affairs, 2020).
2. Delhi Government's Welfare Schemes: Various schemes, such as Muhalla Clinics, focus on improving access to healthcare and social justice for vulnerable communities, promoting inclusive governance at the local level (Delhi Government, 2020).

## *Case Study 2: Jharkhand*

Jharkhand, a state with a significant tribal population, faces challenges related to social justice, human rights, and institutional strength, particularly in terms of ensuring access to justice and combating violence.

**Key Aspects and Challenges**

1. Violence and Human Rights: Jharkhand is prone to violence driven by Naxalite insurgency and inter-communal conflicts. Human rights violations, especially against Scheduled Tribes (STs), are significant challenges. The issue of land rights for indigenous communities and displacement due to mining activities remains a core concern (Jharkhand Human Rights Commission, 2020).

2. Social Justice: Jharkhand has introduced several initiatives aimed at improving the welfare of Scheduled Tribes, but the implementation of policies related to land rights and economic empowerment remains inconsistent (State Government of Jharkhand, 2020).

3. Access to Justice: The judicial system in Jharkhand struggles with backlogs and delays, though initiatives like e-Courts are improving efficiency. However, legal awareness and accessibility remain limited in rural areas (National Judicial Data Grid, 2020).

**Policies and Initiatives**

1. Jharkhand State Legal Services Authority (JHALSA): JHALSA has been at the forefront of providing free legal aid and conducting legal literacy camps for marginalized communities. This initiative is crucial for improving access to justice in remote and underserved areas (Jharkhand State Legal Services Authority, 2020).

2. Tribal Welfare Initiatives: The state has implemented policies under the Tribal Sub-Plan to uplift Scheduled Tribes through education, employment, and land rights

reforms. However, challenges remain in ensuring the equitable distribution of these benefits (Ministry of Tribal Affairs, 2020).

## *Case Study 3: Odisha*

Odisha, located in eastern India, is known for its natural disasters, which impact peace, justice, and institutional governance. However, it has made significant strides in improving governance and addressing social justice issues.

**Key Aspects and Challenges**

1. Violence and Social Justice: Odisha has made significant progress in tackling gender-based violence, particularly through the State Commission for Women. However, violence against women, children, and marginalized groups continues to be a challenge (State Commission for Women, Odisha, 2020).

2. Corruption: Odisha has faced issues of corruption, particularly in public works and natural resource management, which impacts the effectiveness of governance (Anti-Corruption Bureau, Odisha, 2021). Transparency in the allocation of resources and execution of development projects remains a priority.

3. Disaster Preparedness: Odisha's vulnerability to cyclones and floods has made disaster preparedness and response a key focus area. The State Disaster Management Authority (SDMA) has worked to build robust disaster resilience frameworks, which has enhanced Odisha's institutional capacity for responding to crises (Odisha State Disaster Management Authority, 2020).

**Policies and Initiatives**

1. Odisha State Legal Services Authority (OSLSA): This authority works to ensure that citizens, especially the economically weaker sections, have access to legal services and justice. Through the promotion of legal awareness campaigns, OSLSA addresses issues of social justice (OSLSA Report, 2020).

2. Disaster Resilience and Early Warning Systems: Odisha has developed effective early warning systems and community-based disaster management frameworks. These initiatives contribute significantly to building institutional resilience, especially in the context of natural disasters like cyclones and floods (National Disaster Management Authority [NDMA], 2020).

## *Recommendations and Best Practices from Other States and UTs*

1. Community-Based Justice Initiatives: States like Kerala have pioneered community justice initiatives that could be adapted in Delhi, Jharkhand, and Odisha to strengthen access to justice at the grassroots level. Kerala's People's Plan Campaign has empowered communities to participate in local governance and decision-making, contributing to peace and justice (Government of Kerala, 2020).

2. Digital Governance and Transparency: The e-Governance initiatives in Andhra Pradesh and Rajasthan have demonstrated the importance of digital tools in enhancing transparency and reducing corruption. These

models can be replicated in other states to improve institutional transparency and efficiency (Andhra Pradesh e-Governance Report, 2020).

3. Strengthening Institutional Capacity for Disaster Management: Odisha's success in disaster preparedness, such as State Disaster Response Teams (SDRT) and community-based disaster management plans, can serve as a model for other states vulnerable to natural disasters, including Jharkhand and Delhi (NDMA, 2020).

## Conclusion

The states of Delhi, Jharkhand, and Odisha have made substantial progress towards achieving SDG 16, though challenges remain, particularly in reducing violence, ensuring equal access to justice, and improving the functioning of institutions. By implementing community-driven approaches, leveraging digital tools for transparency, and strengthening institutional capacities, these states have made notable strides in improving peace, justice, and strong institutions. Best practices from other states, such as Kerala's community justice model and Odisha's disaster resilience framework, offer valuable lessons that can be applied to enhance the overall effectiveness of governance and institutional frameworks across India.

# SDG 17 – Partnerships for the Goals

The 17th Sustainable Development Goal, "Partnerships for the Goals," emphasizes the need for global collaboration to achieve sustainable development. Partnerships between governments, private sectors, civil society, and international organizations are pivotal to achieving the ambitious targets set by the 2030 Agenda. This chapter delves into the role of partnerships in driving progress on

SDG 17, with a particular focus on India's national strategies, community-led initiatives, and integration with global efforts. It also highlights best practices from other countries to provide a roadmap for effective collaborations.

## Key Indicators and Challenges

SDG 17 encompasses diverse indicators that measure the success of partnerships. These include financial resource mobilization, technology transfer, capacity-building, trade, and systemic coherence in achieving sustainable development. India has shown progress in several areas. For instance, the SDG India Index 2023-2024 reveals advancements in financial inclusion and international trade partnerships. However, gaps persist, especially in areas such as access to technology and resource mobilization for marginalized regions (NITI Aayog, 2023).

The mobilization of financial resources remains a critical challenge. Public-private partnerships (PPPs) have been instrumental in addressing infrastructure needs, but their implementation is uneven across sectors and states. Moreover, the COVID-19 pandemic exposed vulnerabilities in global and regional partnerships, disrupting trade, supply chains, and healthcare collaborations. These disruptions underscore the need for resilient partnerships that can withstand future shocks.

## National Policies and Frameworks

India's policy framework to strengthen partnerships for sustainable development is robust. The Ministry of External Affairs, in collaboration with NITI Aayog and other government bodies, plays a pivotal role in fostering international partnerships. The International Solar Alliance (ISA), launched in 2015, exemplifies India's leadership in forging global coalitions for renewable energy. With over

120 member countries, the ISA seeks to mobilize $1 trillion in investments for solar energy by 2030, significantly contributing to SDG 7 while reinforcing SDG 17.

India's proactive leadership in declaring 2023 as the International Year of Millets at the United Nations General Assembly reflects its commitment to addressing global food security and nutrition challenges. Millets, often termed "nutri-cereals," are climate-resilient and nutrient-rich, making them a sustainable choice for addressing hunger and malnutrition (SDG 2). Through this initiative, India has successfully encouraged nations to adopt millet farming practices and incorporate these grains into national diets, thus promoting biodiversity and sustainable agricultural practices (NITI Aayog, 2023).

Domestically, initiatives such as the Aspirational Districts Programme (ADP) focus on improving socio-economic indicators in underdeveloped districts through coordinated efforts by central and state governments, private players, and non-governmental organizations (NGOs). This program's multi-stakeholder approach ensures the alignment of resources and expertise to uplift marginalized communities (NITI Aayog, 2023).

From a national perspective, India has strengthened its digital governance capabilities, contributing to SDG 9 (Industry, Innovation, and Infrastructure) and SDG 17. The Aadhaar-based Direct Benefit Transfer (DBT) system, now a model for many countries, ensures transparency and reduces corruption in welfare schemes. Countries in Africa and Asia have shown interest in replicating this model to streamline public service delivery (Economic and Political Weekly, 2023).

India's trade policies also reflect its commitment to SDG 17. By enhancing trade agreements and promoting exports,

India has strengthened its position in global markets. The Regional Comprehensive Economic Partnership (RCEP) negotiations, although not finalized, indicate India's intent to integrate with global trade frameworks. Additionally, the focus on digital trade and e-commerce partnerships has opened new avenues for collaboration in the technology sector (Ministry of Commerce, 2023).

India's focus on vaccine equity during the COVID-19 pandemic showcased its role as a responsible global partner. Through initiatives like Vaccine Maitri, India provided over 250 million vaccine doses to more than 100 countries, including underprivileged nations in Africa and the Caribbean, bolstering global health resilience and reinforcing SDG 3. This initiative exemplified the spirit of global solidarity during a critical juncture in public health history (Ministry of External Affairs, 2022).

India has also taken strides in fostering south-south cooperation through the India-UN Development Partnership Fund, operational in more than 40 developing countries. This initiative supports projects in areas such as climate resilience, healthcare, and sustainable livelihoods, strengthening its role as a partner in advancing equitable development globally (UNDP, 2023).

In addition, India's cultural diplomacy has become a significant tool for strengthening partnerships for global goals. The country's focus on Ayurveda and traditional medicine has found global traction, with countries like Japan, Germany, and the United States integrating these practices into their healthcare systems. This aligns with SDG 3, as traditional medicine promotes preventive healthcare while fostering cross-cultural exchange. One of India's globally recognized initiatives is the promotion of International Yoga Day, celebrated annually on June 21.

Proposed by India and endorsed by the United Nations in 2014, International Yoga Day has seen participation from over 190 countries, emphasizing holistic health and well-being, directly aligning with SDG 3 (Good Health and Well-Being). This initiative not only underscores India's soft power but also promotes global awareness about preventive healthcare and mental well-being (United Nations, 2014).

Further reinforcing its partnerships, India has emphasized gender equality on global platforms. Initiatives like the Women's Leadership Forum under the G20 presidency have spotlighted women's roles in leadership, entrepreneurship, and policymaking. This initiative aligns closely with SDG 5 (Gender Equality) and aims to create a network of empowered women leaders globally.

## Community Initiatives

Grassroots-level partnerships have proven to be effective in addressing local challenges. Self-Help Groups (SHGs) across India have played a transformative role in empowering women and marginalized communities. In Kerala, Kudumbashree, one of the world's largest women's collectives, integrates economic empowerment with social development, showcasing the power of local partnerships.

In Rajasthan, the watershed development program illustrates how partnerships between local communities, government bodies, and NGOs can rejuvenate natural resources. This initiative has improved water availability, boosted agricultural productivity, and fostered community resilience against climate change (NIRDPR, 2023).

## Global Best Practices

Global examples provide valuable insights into fostering effective partnerships. Norway's emphasis on technology transfer through international collaborations has accelerated renewable energy adoption in developing countries. Similarly, Germany's Marshall Plan with Africa focuses on building equitable trade partnerships, enhancing skill development, and promoting infrastructure investments in African nations.

Closer to home, Bangladesh's "Digital Bangladesh" initiative demonstrates the transformative potential of technology-driven partnerships. By integrating private sector expertise and government policies, this initiative has improved access to digital services, education, and healthcare, aligning with multiple SDGs, including SDG 17.

## *Recommendations*

To further strengthen partnerships, India must prioritize specific strategies. Firstly, enhancing resource mobilization through innovative financial instruments, such as green bonds and impact investments, can bridge funding gaps. Expanding technology transfer agreements and fostering collaborations in research and development (R&D) are equally critical to addressing technological disparities.

Public-private partnerships should be streamlined with clear regulatory frameworks to ensure equitable resource distribution. Emphasizing transparency and accountability in PPP projects can enhance their effectiveness. Moreover, integrating local governments and community organizations into national and international partnerships will ensure inclusivity and sustainability.

Learning from global best practices, India can adapt Germany's approach to equitable trade partnerships and

Norway's emphasis on technology transfer to local contexts. Strengthening regional partnerships within South Asia through SAARC or BIMSTEC platforms can also amplify collective progress toward the SDGs.

## *Conclusion*

Achieving SDG 17 requires a concerted effort from all stakeholders—governments, private sectors, civil societies, and international organizations. India's initiatives, from the Aspirational Districts Programme to international coalitions like the ISA, underscore the importance of partnerships in sustainable development. By addressing existing gaps and drawing on global best practices, India can pave the way for a collaborative and resilient future. The essence of SDG 17 lies in unity and shared responsibility, reinforcing the idea that global challenges demand collective solutions.

# CHAPTER EIGHTEEN

# References

Alabi, R. O., and A. M. Alabi. 2014. "Socioeconomic Factors Influencing Girls' Education in Developing Countries: A Case Study of Rural Nigeria." International Journal of Educational Development 39: 1-9.

Bano, S. 2017. Gender Disparity in Literacy Levels: A Study of the Awadh Region of Uttar Pradesh. New Delhi: National Publishing House.

Basu, M., S. Pandey, and V. Gupta. 2021. "Maternal Health in India: An Evaluation of Janani Suraksha Yojana." Health Policy and Planning 36(1): 45-57.

Chaudhary, N. 2020. "Beti Bachao Beti Padhao: A Reality Check." Journal of Gender Studies 29(2): 112-127.

Dostie, B., and M. Jayaraman. 2006. "The Impact of Parental Education on Child Enrollment in School: Evidence from India." World Development 34(10): 1562-1576.

Gitonga, E. 2009. "Social Barriers to Girls' Education in Uttar Pradesh." Journal of Gender Studies 17(2): 156-168.

Hickey, S., and M. Startton. 2007. "The Parental Attitudes Toward Girls' Education in Rural Uttar Pradesh." International Journal of Sociology 35(4): 24-39.

Kumar, R., and A. Mishra. 2019. "Financial Literacy and Sukanya Samriddhi Yojana: Challenges and Opportunities."

International Journal of Economics and Finance 11(3): 58-70.

Latha, M. 2014. "The Challenges to Female Education in Uttar Pradesh: Gender and Socioeconomic Inequalities." Asian Education and Development Studies 3(2): 112-130.

Masculinity, Intimate Partner Violence, and Son Preference in India – Findings from Uttar Pradesh. 2023. International Journal of Social Issues.

Menon, S., V. Rao, and P. Singh. 2020. "One Stop Centres in India: Evaluating Their Effectiveness in Addressing Violence Against Women." Indian Journal of Social Work 81(4): 532-548.

Mishra, P., and R. Gupta. 2022. "Kasturba Gandhi Balika Vidyalaya: Bridging the Gender Gap in Education." Asian Journal of Education 41(3): 237-252.

Nair, S. 2020. "Assessing the Impact of Pradhan Mantri Mudra Yojana on Women Entrepreneurs in India." Indian Economic Review 45(2): 211-230.

Rao, P. 2021. "Challenges in Women's Helpline Services: An Analysis of 181." Journal of Public Policy 56(1): 78-90.

Shahidul, H., and N. Karim. 2015. "Infrastructural Challenges to Girl's Education in Rural India." Global Journal of Educational Research 14(3): 45-58.

Sharma, R. 2021. "Encouraging Women in STEM: A Study of Pragati Scholarship Scheme." Journal of Educational Development 12(1): 59-70.

Reports and Publications:

Department of Drinking Water and Sanitation. Annual Report 2020-21. Ministry of Jal Shakti, Government of India.

Ministry of Environment, Forests and Climate Change. Climate Change Vulnerability Assessment for Rajasthan. Government of India, 2020.

NITI Aayog. India SDG Index 2020. Government of India.

National Institute of Rural Development. Water Management and Gender Issues in Rajasthan. 2020.

Rajasthan State Government. Rajasthan Water Sector Restructuring Project Report 2020.

Swachh Bharat Mission (SBM). Progress Report 2020. Government of India.

NITI Aayog. India SDG Index 2023. New Delhi: NITI Aayog, 2023.

Ministry of Labour and Employment. Periodic Labour Force Survey 2022-23. New Delhi: Ministry of Labour and Employment, 2023.

Reserve Bank of India. State Finances: A Study of Budgets 2023-24. Mumbai: RBI, 2023.

Ministry of Electronics and IT. Digital India Annual Report 2023. New Delhi: MeitY, 2023.

Startup India. Startup Ecosystem in India: Report 2024. New Delhi: Startup India, 2024.

World Bank. India Development Update 2023: Jobs and Growth. Washington, DC: World Bank, 2023.

International Labour Organization. Decent Work in India: Challenges and Opportunities. Geneva: ILO, 2023.

Delhi Government. Annual Economic Survey 2023-24. New Delhi: Government of Delhi, 2023.

SEWA. Empowering Informal Workers in Urban India. New Delhi: SEWA, 2024.

Reserve Bank of India. State Finances: A Study of Budgets 2023-24. Mumbai: RBI, 2024.

Ministry of Rural Development. MGNREGA Impact Assessment 2023. New Delhi: Ministry of Rural Development, 2023.

Ministry of Commerce and Industry. Ease of Doing Business Report 2024. New Delhi: Ministry of Commerce and Industry, 2024.

Ministry of Power. Hydropower Development in Arunachal Pradesh. New Delhi: Ministry of Power, 2024.

World Bank. Sustainable Infrastructure in Northeastern India. Washington, DC: World Bank, 2024.

Ministry of Environment, Forest and Climate Change. Environmental Impact of Industrial Projects 2024. New Delhi: MoEFCC, 2024.

Ministry of Transport. Infrastructure Development in the Northeast 2024. New Delhi: Ministry of Transport, 2024.

Ministry of New and Renewable Energy. Annual Renewable Energy Report 2023. New Delhi: MNRE, 2023.

Government of Arunachal Pradesh. State Industrial Policy 2022. Arunachal Pradesh, 2022.

Government of Tripura. Bamboo Mission Progress Report 2024. Tripura, 2024.

Ministry of Statistics and Programme Implementation. Social Indicators India 2023. New Delhi: MoSPI, 2023.

Ministry of Health and Family Welfare. National Health Profile 2023. New Delhi: MoHFW, 2023.

UNDP. Human Development Report 2023. New York: United Nations Development Programme, 2023.

Government of Rajasthan. Bhamashah Yojana Annual Report 2024. Jaipur: Government of Rajasthan, 2024.

Government of Mizoram. Economic Development Report 2024. Aizawl: Government of Mizoram, 2024.

International Labour Organization (ILO). World Employment Social Outlook 2023. Geneva: ILO, 2023.

Ministry of Housing and Urban Affairs. Annual Report 2023-24. New Delhi: MoHUA, 2023.

World Bank. India Development Update 2023. Washington, D.C.: World Bank, 2023.

Ministry of Housing and Urban Affairs. Pradhan Mantri Awaas Yojana Report 2023. New Delhi: MoHUA, 2023.

Ministry of Statistics and Programme Implementation. Housing and Urban Development Statistics 2023. New Delhi: MoSPI, 2023.

North Eastern Region Urban Development Programme. Progress Report 2023. Aizawl: NERUDP, 2023.

Ministry of Transport. FAME II Implementation Report. New Delhi: Ministry of Transport, 2023.

MoEFCC. State of Environment Report 2023. New Delhi: MoEFCC, 2023.

RBI. Urban Infrastructure Status Report. Mumbai: Reserve Bank of India, 2023.

Ministry of Statistics and Programme Implementation (MoSPI). SDG India Index 2023.

Central Pollution Control Board (CPCB). Annual Report 2022–2023.

NITI Aayog. Sustainable Development Goals Dashboard 2023.

Economic and Political Weekly. Articles on Resource Management and Inequality.

Reserve Bank of India (RBI). Fiscal Incentives for Sustainable Development, 2023.

Goa Tourism Department. Tourism Statistics and Policy Reports, 2023.

Delhi Urban Shelter Improvement Board. Annual Report, 2023.

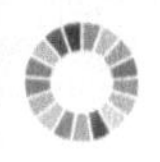


SUSTAINABLE DEVELOPMENT GOALS
1 NO POVERTY
2 ZERO HUNGER
3 GOOD HEALTH AND WELL-BEING
4 QUALITY EDUCATION
5 GENDER EQUALITY
6 CLEAN WATER AND SANITATION
7 AFFORDABLE AND CLEAN ENERGY
8 DECENT WORK AND ECONOMIC GROWTH
9 INDUSTRY, INNOVATION AND INFRASTRUCTURE
10 REDUCED INEQUALITIES
11 SUSTAINABLE CITIES AND COMMUNITIES
12 RESPONSIBLE CONSUMPTION AND PRODUCTION
13 CLIMATE ACTION
14 LIFE BELOW WATER
15 LIFE ON LAND
16 PEACE, JUSTICE AND STRONG INSTITUTIONS
17 PARTNERSHIPS FOR THE GOALS